Voiceovers

Techniques and Tactics for Success

Janet Wilcox

**ALLWORTH
PRESS**
NEW YORK

D0967448

11 10 09   5 4 3 2

Published by Allworth Press
An imprint of Allworth Communications, Inc.
10 East 23rd Street, New York, NY 10010

Cover design by Derek Bacchus
Interior design by Mary Belibasakis
Page composition/typography by Integra Software Services, Pvt., Ltd., Pondicherry, India
Cover photo by © image100

Library of Congress Cataloging-in-Publication Data

Wilcox, Janet.
  Voiceovers : techniques and tactics for success / Janet Wilcox.
    p.   cm.
  Includes index.
  ISBN-13: 978-1-58115-475-7 (pbk.)
  ISBN-10: 1-58115-475-5 (pbk.)
1. Television announcing.   2. Radio announcing.   3. Voice-overs.   I. Title.

  PN1992.8.A6W55 2007
  791.4502'8023—dc22

                                                              2006032404

Printed in Canada

Contents

Preface

When a movie star walks down the street he is likely to be followed by an entourage, fans, and the paparazzi. An equally talented voice-over artist, on the other hand, usually remains invisible, no matter how successful she's been. However, once people discover that she's a voice-over artist, she's in the limelight.

"What kind of jobs do you do?"

"Do I have the right kind of voice to do it?"

"How much money do you make?"

These are the questions that are likely to follow.

I discovered voice acting on my first production job at HBO. I was hooked after my initial recording in the booth. I studied, acted, and booked everything from spots to shows. These shows have included E! Network's *Hollywood & Divine, Beauty Secrets Revealed*. I was also the voice of Lifetime TV's Billboards. This experience and my academic background were a perfect match for University of California, Los Angeles (UCLA) Extension.

Once I started teaching at UCLA Extension, I was surprised that so many people told me they were interested in pursuing voice-overs or taking my class. Then I realized that there are many people who want to test the waters and see if the field is right for them; but they're too busy to get to a class or don't want to invest too much money at first.

I created this book for these curious people, including actors wanting to transfer their skills or anyone who has been told that they have a nice voice. This book can be used as a personal study guide, or for a class, or study group. The book is intended to be a voice-acting method book to set a strong foundation for work in the recording studio. I have organized the genres and exercises in a sequential pattern to build skills up to a greater level of difficulty. There is, however, no reason why a more experienced voice actor can't pick and choose what he or she wants to work on, in any order.

Acting Comes First

The competition for voice-over jobs is very stiff—especially nowadays, when celebrities are eager to do voices for products, to narrate documentaries, and to create bigger-than-life cartoon characters. My goal in writing this book is to help the aspiring non-celebrity voice actor to strengthen the acting technique that is needed to compete in a market that requires believable characters. Truthful acting has to be at the core of all work. And in order to get to this core, I am going to utilize a game-playing theme to get the creative juices flowing. Improvisation has influenced my work in everything from my live announcing gig for AMC's *Nicole Kidman, An American Cinematheque Tribute*, to the narration of my children's book, *Fifi of Fifth Avenue* (featuring twenty-nine characters).

Thinking out of the box helped me write and produce promos for HBO and A&E. I found flexibility crucial for directing celebrities as varied as Jerry Seinfeld and Gladys Knight. Finally, I discovered that fast, free-flowing thinking was essential to meeting the varied needs of my students at UCLA Extension. In sum, improvisation has inspired me in every area of the voice-over industry.

Speaking of "every area of the industry," there are many opportunities in voice-overs, such as: *commercials, infomercials, trailers, promos, looping, adr, dubbing, phone prompts, Internet audio, A/V presentations, documentaries, video games, audio books, point-of-purchase displays, industrials, marketing tapes, Web sites, toys, museums, animated TV shows, DVDs, feature films, pods, and cell phones.* These jobs may garner fifty dollars or thousands of dollars for a few hours of work. I've focused on the areas that I believe can enhance the range of a voice actor and yield decent pay or pleasure for an hour in the booth.

The book starts out with an overview of basic techniques and the industry. Then more and more exercises are introduced as different industry genres and jobs are discussed. Finally, business tips and advice from industry experts address etiquette and successful career moves. You can turn to the appendix for scripts and all of the checklists.

This book is all about playing the game to win and the only way to do that is to have fun. You'll learn the rules of the game with exercises. Then you can get an idea how to play the game as you read stories about jobs from professionals in the business. And, finally, you'll understand how to cash in and win with your first paycheck. When was the last time you played a game and enjoyed it?

Turn the page and let the games begin.

1

The Rules of the Game

*A*re you willing to lose your inhibitions and let your voice soar to new heights? Then get ready to play to win the game of voice-over. It requires fast thinking and the ability to quickly *make-believe*. You have to be excellent to be asked to play this game. Just like when you play a video game, you've got to be engaged with full-on concentration and you may have to play it over and over again to reach your goal.

Keep a playful attitude as you begin to do the exercises in this book. Play them with the same determination you use with interactive games. This book can be treated like an online course, but without the computer. In addition, you can study with me on the Internet. You can also do phone lessons. Just go to my Web site at *www.janetwilcox.com* and e-mail me for rates if you're interested in taking lessons. Throughout this book, you'll also be given a variety of Web resources to expand your knowledge at your own pace.

The goal in voice-over is to have a free-flowing imagination. You may not have the benefit of a scene partner like on stage or screen (unless you're doing multiple character work). You may have to imagine you're speaking to a real person, rather than standing in a booth and talking in front of a microphone. You don't have to learn lines but you have to work quickly. Your ability to imagine you're in the moment, in a real scene, makes or breaks your performance.

All actors must be creative, but the voice-over artist has to rely on their imagination to make-believe they're engaged in activities. You don't have the benefit of a lot of movement because you have to stay in front of the mic—everything comes from your mind's eye. Senses like hearing, tasting, touching, and scent come from your imagination. Your emotional needs and motivations have to be as real as any scene in real life. At the same time you have to remain glued to the script because you're reading. Therefore, the goal is to meld your mind's eye with the page.

You can build these skills with practice. Improv is an excellent model to use in this medium because it helps build the *imagination muscle*. It also helps you respond spontaneously. One of the myths about improv is that it comes without work. This is not true. If you perform in an improv show, you constantly practice games and exercises. In the same way, you must constantly train yourself to be ready for the quick responses required in voice-over.

The idea is that you practice so much that you can virtually pick up a script and bring it to life. You simulate situations in your home workouts so that your imagination muscle and read-aloud skills are strong.

From the start, I encourage you to be patient as you practice the indepth acting exercises. I've included a series of basic acting lessons so you can build a solid foundation for voice-over work, especially if you're a beginner. My class at UCLA Extension is twelve weeks long, so you may consider doing the exercises over twelve weeks or longer. It is essential to acquire a strong acting background because you will have little time to prepare for voice-over jobs and auditions. Spontaneity and creativity are the keys to bringing voice-over copy to life.

Developing a strong, consistent workout is crucial in building a successful voice-over career. Even if you are taking lessons or doing private coaching, you need to work on your own. During those times when you're not studying with someone, you have to be even more diligent!

This book is the perfect way to test the waters at your own pace and decide what your next step should be to pursue your voice-over career.

But first take a little quiz to see what you know and where you stand in the field.

VOICE-OVER QUIZ	T	F
I believe I'll make a lot of money doing voice-over:		
I believe I could start doing it right now:		
Everybody always told me I had a nice voice:		
I don't know anybody in the business so I'll never make it:		
I can quit my day job after I book my first job:		
Voice-over is only for celebrities:		
I can do funny voices and that's all it takes:		

ESTABLISHED SKILLS YOU HAVE (Check Each That Applies):	
Acting	
Singing	
On-camera commercial	
Theater	
Improv	
Stand-up comedy	
Speech competitions	
Film and TV acting	
Read aloud in public a lot (for example at church or to children in a library)	
Voice recording	

Now keep this and review it at the end of the book. You should get a notebook that you can use as a journal to record your growth throughout your workouts. Use this to chart your progress. *Please refer to the appendix for scripts, Web addresses, and specific checklists* that are mentioned in the forthcoming chapters.

Pre-Game

I was inspired to pursue voice-overs on my first production job at HBO when my boss said, "Janet, you have a nice voice, why don't you read this?" After that, years of study and hard work as an actress paid off and I booked wonderful jobs, including my weekly gig as the voice of Lifetime's Billboards. As I was building my voice-over career, I wrote, produced, and directed promos for HBO and A&E in New York City. These two career paths and my teaching experience at Marymount Manhattan College led me to UCLA Extension when my husband's career took off and my family moved to the West Coast.

When I moved to Los Angeles, I had to make many transitions. I had to work on getting my home studio up and running and had to prepare to teach my class at UCLA Extension. How could I take my twenty years of voice-over experience and condense it into a twelve-week course? The answers came when I drew on the principles I learned from Paul Sills, the great improv guru who was a co-founder of Chicago's Compass Players and The Second City. I integrated improv games to exemplify concepts and help students become free and relaxed.

Paul Sills said that his game playing techniques could be taught to anyone. I think it is because everyone loves to be playful. Even as adults, we've all pretended to do things in everyday life. We might pretend to be on the phone to avoid talking with someone, for example.

The Clock Is Running

In 2004, prior to the Olympic games in Greece, the voice of James Earl Jones resonated magnificently in the introduction over the opening montage on NBC. His voice-over heralded the epic spirit of the games. Viewers were once again treated to the inimitable voice of CNN and Darth Vader.

James Earl Jones is the embodiment of a great voice actor. His acting shines and his voice cuts through clearly, over all music and effects.

Today, celebrities as voice actors abound. They have become synonymous with products and have created captivating roles in animated features; Sally Kellerman made salad dressing sound delicious, Gene Hackman has helped us buy home products, and Christine Lahti has lured us to pamper our skin. Animated roles have attracted many screen stars including Cameron Diaz and Paul Newman. Advertisers benefit from the instant recognition value of famous voice actors.

Noteworthy actors have also created an easy conversational style in voice-overs because they use their natural voices and sound like they are truthfully talking to someone. They make it a dialogue and not a monologue. The reads aren't pushed or fake unless a particular advertising campaign calls for that style. The era of the announcer as the "Voice of God" is over. Therefore, it is important for voice-over artists to use a truthful acting technique to create believable characters in the current voice-over market.

Herein lies the challenge for non-actors. It is important for non-actors to study and practice to replicate this free and easy style. Often, inexperienced actors have to learn to lose inhibitions in order to unearth truthful emotions and create credible characters. In essence, all good actors expose their vulnerabilities; this is what attracts an audience to the performer. The audience and the actor share universal emotions and experiences. It's necessary to master this technique to compete with the actors in Hollywood.

It is naïve to believe anybody can step into the booth and pick up a piece of copy and make it sound like a real conversation. Does this mean you should give up because the competition is too stiff? The answer is no—if you're willing to play and have fun.

However, although the industry is filled with very competitive heavy hitters, the truth is that, at the same time, technology has made it more and more accessible to the masses. As MP3 files are used more and more for home auditions, anyone with a computer and mic can pay a fee to sign up for Internet casting services. Imagine recording your own voice from home! (I'll discuss these services in greater detail later in the book.)

This proliferation of Internet-based auditions does, however, include non-union work. If you're starting out this is great. You're not in the union and this is a way to get experience. However, veteran performers have paid their dues in the business and unions play an important role in the industry. Unions were created to ensure voice actors would be paid a fair wage in a timely fashion. A fair wage may not always be forthcoming with non-union work. So, you should join the union when it's feasible.

To sum it up, there are opportunities in many places for a voice actor these days. Your success depends largely on your attitude, savvy, and work ethic. Moreover, I believe your will to succeed is linked to your ability to play while you get paid.

The Starting Line

I have compiled this work from my years as a student and professional voice-over artist. Anyone in the performing arts who attempts to pass on what she has learned over a lifetime realizes that her own knowledge owes a debt to the teachers and colleagues she has encountered along the way. Therefore, all attempts have been made to cite teachers or sources of the learning material for further study. In some cases, the knowledge was passed on in many different classes and there is no text reference.

You should use this book as a starting point. Eventually you'll find what works for you when you perform. Please keep in mind that I come from an acting background. *I believe that you are always in a scene talking to one person when you perform voice-overs.* Voice-over is very intimate so it is better to imagine you're talking to one person rather than a group of people when you perform.

You have probably been encouraged to become a voice-over artist. Someone told you that you have a nice voice. As a result of this, you've been asked to read passages or maybe even record a script. All of that was fun but you didn't know how to pursue a voice-over career. Everyone says you'll make a lot of money. What's more, people say it's easy and doesn't take any time, or, it would seem, talent.

Well, as with everything, you should take this with a grain of salt. The good news is that everyone is right. You can have fun and make money. However, you have to learn the rules of the game to succeed.

Getting a Feel for the Playing Field

If you love sports, you'll always want to continue to play because it's just plain fun. The same idea can be applied to voice acting. If you treat a career like a game you will always win big. When I studied with Paul Sills, he interspersed children's games such as Red Light, Green Light between improv exercises to help keep the class lively and fun. But even a simple game like Red Light, Green Light has all the elements that make it a perfect example of how games are structured and why that structure is so applicable to improvisational acting. The game has a goal—to make it all the way up to the guy who is saying "Red light," touch him on the back, and then run back to the starting line before he catches you. It has rules—you can only move when the guy doesn't see you; if he does see you, he can send you back to the starting line, he has to keep his back turned to the other players when he is counting, he isn't allowed to turn around without saying "red light," and he isn't allowed to tag you if you get back "home" safely. As long as you stay within those rules, you can do anything you want to achieve your goal. The game also has stakes; you could win or you could lose. Although the consequences of losing are not severe, the fact that you have to make immediate, spontaneous decisions in order to stay in the game make the game suspenseful, and therefore, fun.

If you think about it, this "game theory" is applicable to auditions, too, because an audition is much like a game. You're given only bits and pieces of information—those pieces of information are the equivalent of your "rules." You have to *fill in the blanks*. It's like answering *twenty questions* as you build your character. You have to make decisions about who this person is from a few clues. It's almost like a *scavenger hunt* as you search for treasures in the script that will help you piece your scene together and lead you to a prize booking.

If you want to be a working voice actor, the first thing you have to do is to strengthen your acting skills.

Here are some basic rules that will help you win the voice-over game.

You Must Have Excellent Breath Control

Breath control requires constant practice to increase and expand your ability to do fast and slow reads. It also requires good body alignment to allow the breath to flow freely. Pilates can be a useful tool to create good posture. Osteopaths often help correct some imperfections to increase airflow. It is also important to do exercises so you can monitor your breathing capacity. Singing, of course, is a great way to complement this work, if you study with a competent teacher.

Even more important though is that you *check in* on your breathing patterns, so you can avoid shallow breathing or holding your breath. Auditions can be nerve racking (if you let them be). It's important to always keep breathing through the silly, self-imposed fear actors experience in auditions.

You Need Control of All Parts of Your Vocal Instrument

Tongue twisters help keep you ready for the difficult copy you'll be given. Constantly working on pitch variation in both singing and speaking will allow you to add interesting inflections to your work. Vocal warm up exercises that release tension in the jaw, tongue, and face are important to create a clean sound. Speech classes and singing classes are wonderful ways to hone this craft.

You Must Have Razor-Sharp Read-Aloud Skills

This means you can make copy sound like conversation. No one wants to pay to hear you read. You must learn to use acting skills to help you sound like you are speaking to someone in a real life situation. The art of reading aloud takes constant practice and monitoring to assure that you sound natural. In addition, some people need to just work on the *technical skill* of reading out loud without making mistakes. It's important to learn to keep your eyes on the page and be in the moment with each word.

While you're working on your reading skills, remember that any piece of copy can be read in endless ways. *You must have good interpretation skills.* If you read the copy like the writer envisioned it and also add your own special style to it, you may book the job. Again, approach this like a game. If you think of yourself as a superhero, here to save the day, then you'll have fun breaking down copy and *playing* with it prior to the audition. Actors who add inspired interpretations to a script fascinate audiences. In a nutshell, this requires a playful imagination that is ready to respond on cue.

You Need to Be Able to Make Choices Very Quickly

You may not have a lot of time to make choices. The basic *who, what, and where* model of improv is useful to apply to quick reads. Actors also build a range of characters when they perform improv, and improv actors have to quickly take direction from an audience. This is helpful because voice actors must respond instantly to a director's comments. Improv can be broad, so it can be useful to bring animated characters to life.

You Must Be Able to Take Direction

All actors have to fulfill the director's vision. You must be able to change your approach to the script as quickly as a sound engineer says, "Take two." Treat a session like a game. The object of the game—just like in the game Red Light, Green Light—is to do whatever the director says. You must leave your overstuffed ego at the door!

You Have to Have a Keen Ear

Listening skills are critical to becoming a successful voice-over artist. Stop right now. What do you hear? Sound is in the traffic, the baby's cry, and the bird's song. Voice actors must constantly listen to life sounds and other voice-over work. Music is used in most voice-over productions. It is a wonderful tool to play with while you prepare to perform a script.

Let the world be your classroom. Listen in on conversations. Hear the emotion behind the words. Listen to the pitch, accents, and silence. Grasp the rhythms of speech. Go home and imitate what you've heard. Do the same with spots on the air; mimic everything from documentaries to cartoons. Pay special attention to the pacing of each genre. Finally, integrate these styles using your own unique creations based on truthful acting.

In addition, listen to what's on the airwaves. Advertising styles change all the time. You need to always be aware of these shifting tides. Is your voice type everywhere? How do celebrities sound on the air versus the *scale* actor? Where do you fit in? Find your voice type and if possible, adapt to new trends in the industry.

You Need Impeccable Timing

Timing is what makes comedy work. It's what you need to make your reads short or long enough. Timing is essential to hitting your mark when you have to match your voice to an existing track to replace a temporary dialogue track. Learn to listen to music and count the beats. If possible, count the rests between the notes so you get a sense of coming into the flow of an ongoing prerecorded track.

Watch comedians and listen to get a sense of how timing makes or breaks a joke. Conversely, be aware of the pregnant pause in dramatic scenes. Next, listen to the comedic and dramatic timings of voice-overs. Note, for example, how condensed it is for commercials.

You Have to Have a Strong Spirit

Yoga, religion, meditation, and a positive outlook on life can go a long way to build a firm foundation for a voice-over career. Acting taps into the soul. If you are *soulless*, your work will be, too. Audiences respond to that special quality under a performance that connects to something heartfelt or humorous. This requires the actor to have balance in his life.

Constant worrying and obsession in the business can create tension and block the flow of energy. However, if you constantly nourish your soul, you can remain fresh and alive. This game perhaps is the most important one to master.

Julia Cameron's *The Artist's Way* has many excellent exercises to revive the creative spirit. You must constantly feed and nurture your creative side. The more you pamper it, the more it will feed you. Always keep things in perspective. Go to the mountains, sea, or woods. You'll soon realize you're not the most important thing in the universe and your troubles will drift away.

You Must Understand the Genres and Conventions

There are rules that make voice-over styles right or wrong, whether the style is for commercials, promos, or animated shows. Learn these conventions. Also, along the way, take note of your limitations. Perhaps you just can't create enough characters for animation. Maybe you can't sound convincing as a real person in commercials. Whatever you learn, constantly beef up your skills in your weakest area. By building your weakest skills, your signature skills will become even more interesting.

Draw on complementary arts to embellish genres. Read comic strips and children's books; great ways to practice animation skills. Listen to movie star voices for inspiration. Use paintings, movies, theatre, or anything that can complement the genre. It's important to note, however, that you must know the rules of a genre before you can break them. Your game plan is to understand the rules of the medium so well that you'll always win.

You Must Be a Superior Salesperson and Marketer

In order to make it in this business, you have to stand out from the crowd. This is even more the case now as celebrities do a fair share of voice-over work. What makes your voice-over CD pop out in a pile of 1,000 reels? Do you send it in a snazzy package?

Even more important, you must have a marketing plan to get an agent or get work. For example, you may want to market to promo producers to start. You may target small voice-over talent agencies or regional agencies to begin. Perhaps you want to turn acting skills into voice-over skills, and contact agents with that ace card. Write out your strategies. For example, *this month I will seek documentary voice-over work. I'll send out demos and follow up with postcards and phone calls.*

It's good to read books on sales and marketing. Acquire new tricks of the trade. Learn all you can about advertising. The more you know, the more you can meet your client's needs.

In addition, you must have cutting edge tools. Your marketing should stand out with strong visuals and professional packaging, and your voice needs to be recorded on the most current technical format. Years ago voice-over artists used audiotapes—not anymore. Keep pace with the latest technical innovations and be competitive. For example, many professional voice-over artists now have a home recording studio and send auditions via an MP3 file.

In summation, do not just rely on agents to do the work. You should always seek work from other resources. Agents come and go and you should be able to find work on your own during slow periods.

You Must Be a People Person

In real estate, the phrase is, location, location, and location. In voice-over, the phrase should be connections, connections, and connections. The more people you know who can help you, the better. You must be an excellent *people person*. This requires constant work and attention. It also requires sincerity. People see through manipulations. You must work at being personable and likable.

Take people out for drinks or lunch. Join organizations. *Women in Film* is open to women and men in Los Angeles. Volunteer to work in media related organizations to get to know people. You must learn to be resourceful. Search for contacts and jobs on the Web and in magazines. Go to media events and functions. In short—get out there and hustle. It's unlikely you'll be *discovered* practicing voice-over in your home!

Build a good strong network of friends to support your career. It's important to have people to cheer you on when you want to give up. Create a safety net of individuals who will be there to catch you when you fall. In contrast, avoid or ignore individuals who tell you that you'll never succeed.

Play the Game to Win

Practice consistently, even when the business is slow; make a game out of it so that your home workouts are never boring. Love what you do so it never becomes a job. Create a game out of the *drudgery* of voice-over jobs to keep fresh.

For example, the company's future rests in your hands. If you don't show up, people will lose their jobs. Keep raising the bar so you enjoy your quest for higher goals. Tackle different genres such as books, poetry, and plays to add variety to the work.

Expect the Unexpected

This is something like Murphy's Law and it is always true in voice acting: expect the unexpected. What does this mean? Well, for example, expect that your audition will run late. At the same time, expect that you will be late because of traffic, lack of parking, or a subway running late (and tardiness is never kosher). Expect the casting director to ask for a totally different direction than what you have prepared. Expect different copy than what you were given at an audition. Expect plenty of handwritten changes to your script on any given job.

In the end the most important thing is to believe in yourself. Believe that you can do this, you should do this, and that you will do this work. Visualize yourself at the microphone. Keep seeing the image of yourself doing the work. If you believe it can happen, have talent, and work hard—it will happen.

Get Ready for Workouts and Work

It's important to understand that all the workout exercises in this book help you prepare for work but when you do jobs, you can't dwell on these techniques. It's like when you go on stage, you can't think about your lines, you have to jump into a scene you believe is real. I've created these warm-ups so you can take the time to be a better actor before you start to work. Veteran actor Bob Bergen currently does the voice of Porky Pig and he teaches. He stresses the importance of the acting craft for animation work.

Bob Bergen: "As an animation VO teacher, I'm not an acting teacher. My job is to take your acting skills, combine them with the technique of animation, and marry the two into creating characters. This is why I tell people to make sure they are solid actors *before* studying voice-over, even commercial VO . . . But most people don't understand or see the necessity of acting in voice-over. There are those who say to me, 'People always tell me what a great voice I have!' There's no such thing as a great voice, because there's no such thing as a bad voice. There are only good and bad actors."

Personal Workout—Timing Exercises

▶ You'll need to use a clock that counts off seconds for this. First, you will use a small ball, like a tennis ball, and toss it up every five seconds. Don't throw it too high because you'll have to catch it and throw it again right away. Next, toss it up every ten seconds; finally, throw it every fifteen seconds.

▶ Now take something simple to read from a magazine ad and record your work. Use a stopwatch or look at your clock with the second hand just as you start to read. But keep your eyes on the page as you read and stop when you think you've read fifteen seconds. Check your clock or stopwatch and see how you did. Keep practicing until you get it right. Continue to practice the same technique, trying to read in ten and five seconds. Listen back and see if your reading is natural or forced. Is your focus on the time or on the conversation you should be having? You have to internalize timings until they are second nature. This takes practice.

So take advantage of the flexible time you have at home to create a foundation of acting for your voice-over work. As you become more proficient with the basic acting skills, and continue to study, you will be able to make the fast choices necessary for voice-over. In essence, these techniques will be tacit and you won't have to think about them. You may often only have time to use a quick sketch improv model at auditions and jobs. So you must build a stockpile of acting choices to draw on for your performances.

2

Train to Reach Your Fighting Weight

*E*very great athlete trains and trains to be ready for the big event. A voice-over artist is no different. Every job poses new and specific challenges. You have to be at your best whether you're preparing for an animation job or pacing yourself for a live announcer performance.

Vocal artists must always be rested to sound their best. You are an instrument and you need to be very fit. The mind and body need rest for vocal work to perform at an optimal level. In my experience, the first thing that goes is the voice when you are getting sick.

If you're the type who likes to burn both ends of the candle or party late, you'd better change that. Don't believe me? Experiment: record yourself on a day when you've had the least amount of sleep and then do it when you have the most amount of sleep. How do you feel and sound? Of course if you're young, you're bound to have more resilience. Either way, play by the rules. Get consistent good rest especially the night before a gig.

You have to be willing to follow the rules of training to win. It is important to be very hydrated. You need to drink plenty of room temperature water the day before you record and as needed in your session. Warm water is also good, especially if you're not feeling your best or if your mouth is dry from allergy medications. If the rule is to be hydrated, then it is logical that you should avoid or be conservative with the things that dehydrate the voice, such as alcohol, caffeine, and sugar.

During transition seasons and high allergy times, you may need humidification for your nasal passages. We're all different and some of us may be more prone to irritation and allergies. On the other hand, some voice actors can step up to a mic and sound perfect without any warm-up or special care. As Socrates observed, "know thyself."

Preempt Problems

If congestion is a problem, you may need an air purifier. You may need to do a saline wash in your nasal passages to gently rinse out allergens. You can research this on the Web if you go to *saltaire.com*. If you're lucky enough to live by the ocean, walk along the beach to inhale the ocean air. This may help open your passages.

If you are vocally challenged and under the weather take good care of your instrument. You should take extra precautions if you are hoarse. Ear, Nose, and Throat (ENT) Dr. Randolph Schnitman recommends that you do not gargle or whisper if you are hoarse, because the vocal cords become more irritated if you do. The vibrations of the gargling will irritate the vocal cords. Whispering causes the muscles around the cords to be more tense.

Allergies and constant colds are the enemies of your work. If you are prone to these problems, you'll need a good ENT doctor. You should always show up for work in voice-over, so you have to stay healthy. I know of one case when a voice talent called in sick and soon after was replaced by someone else. In this case, it was time for a change and the absence of the voice-over talent gave the client the perfect opportunity to bring in someone new. It's kind of like the idea in theater that you don't want your understudy to do better than you. On a lighter note, it's the reason why Ted Knight never wanted to take a vacation on the *Mary Tyler Moore Show*.

The aforementioned ideas may force you to change your lifestyle. You will have to decide how much you want to be a voice-over artist. If you constantly live on the edge and are reckless with your body, then so be it. You can't use the full potential of your vocal instrument if you abuse your body; therefore, develop positive health habits in order to perform at your best.

Along with a healthy lifestyle comes exercise to remain fit. Although it's not paramount to be in great shape like a dancer or even an actor, it does help your mental drive and stamina. It's good to have some form of workout integrated into your lifestyle along with a sensible diet.

When all is said and done, of course there will always be days when you're not working at your best. That's when your technique will kick in—all the prep work and professional chops you have will go on automatic pilot.

Like all great athletes, you'll play to win and turn off the negative thoughts that could run you down. Great athletes and Broadway actors perform when they're sick, injured, and mourning a loved one's loss.

Remember the old show biz adage—*the show must go on*. The choice is yours. Be fit and at your fighting weight and win, or lose simply because you lack the discipline to go the distance.

Finding Your Balance

Try to just stand on one foot. How's your balance? I always loved dance because you knew right away if you were *centered*.

Too many actors lose their balance. Uta Hagen talked and wrote about the challenge actors face juggling everything. You've got a career, a survival job, and maybe even a family.

Many students wonder if they should quit their day job. No, No, No! There's no reason to fast-forward your life. You'll know when you can manage to live just on voice-over work. Unless, you're wealthy, you will have to have other means of supporting yourself until you *make it*.

If you're a trained actor, maybe you'll book commercials, film, or TV work. Voice-over will just add to your bag of tricks. However, you must be patient and realize success may not happen overnight. You have to study, work, and keep up a home workout until you get there.

The main point is that you need to be realistic. You don't want to be desperate for work when you go to auditions. At the same time, you want to be rested and relaxed when you go on bookings. It's all about finding a balance. You'll need to find a job that is flexible enough to allow you to go on auditions and bookings. Perhaps you've had a job for a long time and can get the time off you need because of your strong record with the company. Bosses would rather keep good employees than train new ones.

I worked in the business as a promo writer/producer. It gave me some flexibility because I had days when I would edit; I also had a long relationship with many editors. I could leave for an hour to audition or do a session because I always came prepared to my edits. I never abused this privilege so it worked out. There were times when I hired a sub-contractor, if necessary.

Remember you'll need to budget voice-over expenses when you start out. You'll need to study, buy equipment to practice with at home, and create demos. All of these things add up. Therefore sit down and write up a budget to fit your current financial situation. Set goals for future costs and purposes.

In the end, the balancing act should keep you centered. You shouldn't feel drained from doing so many things. Hopefully, you'll start booking more jobs and be able to replace survival jobs with the high hourly wage voice-over work brings. Either way, if you see voice-over as fun, you'll find ways to make it happen.

Gear and Play Things

An accomplished musician will play the best instrument possible. In the same vein, voice-over artist Don LaFontaine records in the best studios with the most sophisticated equipment. He knows how to use his instrument and take advantage of the high-tech gear around him.

What if you're just starting out? Don't you need the high-tech equipment to sound your best? Well, in a perfect world it would be nice to have all the playthings the big boys have. However, it's not entirely necessary to have it all at once.

First, it may not be in your best interest to monitor your work with headphones right away. You may become self-conscious. You don't want to censor yourself when you're starting to record yourself.

Second, you need to work on acting skills, which require imagination, and *getting out of your head* when you start. It's important that you *connect* to a real person or scene partner in an imagined scene and that you make what you're reading believable when you begin to approach copy.

If you step up to a professional mic and fall in love with your own voice then you'll sound like an announcer. I even hear professional radio DJs sound like that when they do commercials. Their *perfect sound* supersedes a connection to the scene they are creating.

Equipment and Your Budget

It's only natural that you'll want to experiment with your voice in a booth. However, you can start out using a simple tape recorder with a condenser mic. The important thing is to lay a strong foundation for truthful work. Audiences always respond to heartfelt work. Technical expertise can be layered on top of it. I survived the harsh world of the comedy clubs in the improv show I performed in because I would be truthful and flexible.

Maybe to start you can only afford a small tape recorder with a condenser mic, and a music stand to hold your copy (you can also use a clip to attach copy to something). You can then plan ahead to buy more equipment. You'll add a mic and mic stand next. You may be able to add a computer program such as Sound Forge (personal computer) or Peak (Macintosh) to record and edit your work. Finally, you'll learn to make MP3s to send demos to prospective clients.

Soundproofing is a wonderful thing to add to the mix. A full-blown studio can be costly but you can start with using just a closet. It has prefab walls you can pad with Auralex, sound blankets, or quilts. You can put cork on the floor, maybe plywood on the top and then a piece of carpet. An expensive studio has a raised (sprung) floor to dampen the reverberation. Wherever you set up, listen first. Try to find the quietest place in your home to set up your recording booth. You may be able to build a booth if you're handy. Sound engineers can give helpful advice if you have any contacts at recording studios. You can purchase pre-made booths such as the Whisper Room (*www.whisperroom.com*). Search the Web for equipment and the best prices. However, always research equipment fully with industry pros before putting down your money. You can learn valuable technical tips in *The Voice Actor's Guide To Home Recording* by Jeffrey P. Fischer and Harlan Hogan.

I first recorded my home workouts with a small audiocassette recorder containing a condenser mic. Then, I got a mic and Teac dual record cassette machine. When I needed to record auditions from home, I was motivated to upgrade my system. I use an AKG mic, M-box, and Pro Tools. I've added Auralex, cork, and carpet to a closet to enhance the acoustics for recording. I can send larger CD quality files (AIF or WAV) via an FTP site. After I edit my tracks, I convert the audio to an MP3 file with iTunes.

Play around with a range of mics. Some pick up sound in a unidirectional pattern and others have a heart shaped or cardioid pattern. Explore the nuances of different models of mics from Sennheiser, Neumann, and AKG at a music store.

Another way to get the feel for the mic is to rent a studio just to see how you sound. Before you jump out of your skin about costs, check around as MP3 auditions have become more prevalent and select studios offer reasonable rates for voice actors (at the time of this printing, some are as little as ten dollars for ten minutes).

In Los Angeles, look for special rates at The Voicecaster (818) 841–5300, and in New York call Full House Productions (212) 645–2228, for special offers. Certainly there must be some place in your market where you can play around in a booth for a reasonable rate. Even if you don't have a job or audition, pretend you do and book the studio. It's good to be your own producer. You'll see why it's so important to be on top of your game and efficient in a booth.

Basic Mic Technique

People can tell you all sorts of things about mic technique, but until you experience it, you won't integrate it into your work. It's kind of like when you hear a song in your head and you don't really know it until you sing it out loud. With this being said, there are some basic rules to consider.

First, you send sound to the copy stand past the mic. This idea of sending sound was demonstrated when I took a class at the Stella Adler studio in New York City. It was a wonderful exercise to enhance my vocal projection. The idea is to learn to send your voice to the exit sign at the back of a theatre, if you do stage acting. To practice this you first send sound to a nearby chair, then to the TV in your apartment, and then to your door. It can also be illustrated by thinking of a friend standing in those places. With this in mind, you adjust your volume and projection as if you were speaking to a person in another room. In contrast, if you imagine speaking to someone face to face, you will reduce your volume and not yell. So practice imagining someone you know is in various places in your home and adjust your sound to reach them. Finally, put that person's face on the mic stand and speak to them there, past the mic. It's really just about simple communication. It's important to get that concept down so you project properly.

A second general rule of thumb is that your mouth is about a hand's distance from the mic. Thirdly, you generally work across a mic and not directly *head on*. An engineer will set up a mic properly in a booth so you will be positioned correctly.

Sometimes there will be a *p-pop* screen to eliminate plosive sounds that can occur with the *B* and *P*. This screen is between the mic and the copy stand and therefore can be in your line of vision. It's usually a mesh metal that you can see through. However, you do have to make an adjustment to see copy with this screen and you need to practice with it. You can see what it looks like if you peruse *pop filters* on *www.sweetwater.com*. A simple rule to use if you don't have a screen is to turn your head slightly off mic to avoid the pop with *Ps* and *Bs*.

Refining Your Sound

With all these general rules in mind, know that everything can be altered with more experience. For example, you can move closer to the mic for a sexy or low, ominous read. However, the closer you get to a mic, the more you'll pick up *mouth sounds.* You'll hear lip smacks and noise if you are dry. Also, smacks may come if you open and close your mouth. Therefore, when you work it's easier to keep the mouth open to avoid these distracting sounds.

I remember my first opera technique teacher telling me to keep my mouth open when I sang. It was hard to do but with practice and concentration it was possible. She would talk about how the great Greek orator, *Demosthenes*, would practice speaking with pebbles in his mouth to improve his articulation. This may be a bit extreme given the cost of dental work these days. However, you can get the feel for this by washing your hands and just inserting your finger lengthwise in your mouth and speaking with some copy for a bit. Next, remove the finger and speak. You should feel your mouth more open and your speech flowing more freely.

Foreign objects may encourage an open mouth but you also want to be aware of jaw tension. *You don't want to develop TMJ or a rigid jaw. It's better to just learn the feeling of having an open mouth when you speak and then move on to using your muscle memory when you work.* Actors always need to use their imagination to make things happen. It's like my first acting teacher said, "Make it happen with focus and concentration."

In short, just learn to relax the jaw and leave it loose and open. As for lip smack sounds, if you take allergy medications you can swish warm water to help relieve dryness and reduce mouth noises. There is also a product called *Salivart* that simulates saliva and you can spray that in your mouth as well. Some people find a few bites from a green apple helpful, too.

Whether you buy a mic and play around with volume, placement, and technique at home or work with a good mic in a studio or classroom doesn't matter. It's important to add mic technique to your work once your foundation acting techniques are secure. Volume, intensity, and vocal intonation give color and texture to a read and you need to know how to make this happen with experimentation in classes and practice sessions.

Remember to have fun, too. Try all sorts of things at the mic to learn your limits so you'll feel comfortable and secure on jobs. The truth is every booth is different and every setup requires different nuances. *You must be flexible.* You may wear headphones to hear your work. Some actors prefer not to wear them. It's good to get experience working with and without them.

The Gold Standard

Before you know it, you'll sound like a pro and want your own professional home recording studio, with a top-notch mic, booth, and ISDN line. ISDN allows you to have a two-way dialogue with another studio in a remote location. A device encodes your voice and decodes a producer's voice remotely. You're given direction, you read, and your voice travels to a remote studio where it is recorded.

You'll probably invest thousands of dollars to set up a professional studio with ISDN. Costs add up by the time you add a mixer (like a Mackie) and ISDN box (like a Telos Zephyr).

On the subject of gear, once you start going on auditions, you may want to pack a few provisions for the road. I always have the following: pencils, tissue paper, water, highlighters, clips (to clip copy up if there are no clips), stopwatch, and reading glasses. (I have allergies and may bring nasal spray and I also bring a tiny book light in case there is low light in the waiting room.)

Whatever sound gear and toys you have, get the most out of them. Keep setting goals and raising the bar and you'll continually reach new heights all the time.

Coming Up for Air

Voice Actress, Bonnie Perkinson, prepares to work with the wrong posture. Her neck is collapsed and reaching forward to the mic. (Photography by Zoia Barrio, shot at Atlantis Group Recording Studio)

Voice Actress, Bonnie Perkinson, prepares to work the right way with a long neck and good posture. (Photography by Zoia Barrio, shot at Atlantis Group Recording Studio)

Voice Actress, Bonnie Perkinson, keeps good alignment as she works at the mic. (Photography by Zoia Barrio, shot at Atlantis Group Recording Studio)

Voice work requires relaxation. Tension in the body and throat can be heard. In the beginning, it's important to take a few minutes to relax the body and breathe. You will find breathing exercises in this section and on the CD that comes with this book.

Breathing is the fuel for vocal work. It's the gas that keeps your motor running. When you first start to work, you need to practice correct breathing. Start out incorrectly: take a short breath in your chest and try to talk. You'll feel that this makes the throat tight. This is not how you want to work. You want to relax your body. Lie on your back with your knees bent. Now breathe naturally. Feel your stomach rise and fall. This is the feeling you need when you stand and sit to support your sound. So take a breath in as your stomach rises and release an *e* sound in this position. Then try it sitting and standing. It will take time to master this so be patient.

Pat Whiteman is a voice teacher and performance coach who also teaches a beginning singing class at UCLA Extension. She demonstrated a fun way to make sure your stomach rises and falls when you lie on your back. *Simply put a book on your belly and push it up.* Remember as the book rises, you take in the air. I've included some of Pat's exercises below because they work so well for beginners. Rather than go into great technical detail, I'd like you to master the feeling of good breath support and use it in your work.

When you study speech and singing, you'll be encouraged to breathe from your *diaphragm.* This means you simply let the body do what it can do naturally without tension, just like you did when you breathed while on your back with your knees bent. So that instead of hiking the shoulders or breathing from your chest, you let the lower abdomen rise to take in the air and let the diaphragm drop to help fully fill the lungs.

You also want air to fill the ribcage area of the back too. It all starts low in the pelvic area as you release the lower abdomen. Think of starting the breath almost at the tip of the tailbone to help get the breath in the lower back, too.

You can play with breathing exercises every day. First, replicate that low supported breath and let the diaphragm move freely. Next, you need to breathe deeply a few times. Now try to take in a breath and repeatedly release a *sh* sound. You should notice how your lower abdomen moves in and out as you create the sound. Do two quick releases of the *sh* sound and then a long one where you release the air slowly and fully. Then relax.

Next, try to take in a good full breath and count out loud to twenty with an even, steady, chant-like pace. Take note of how far you can go and increase it as you practice daily.

Now take a nice big breath in and hold it for two counts and then just let the air expel fully. Do this a few times. Just check in with your low supported breath again and see if you can feel your back expand at the ribs and in the lower back. You can feel this sitting in a straight-back chair. Next, just relax for a minute.

Now imagine that you've got a birthday candle in front of you. You'll take in a breath and slowly release it from the tiniest opening from your lips. The idea behind this standard singing exercise is that you're moving the air very slowly; so slowly that if you had a candle in front of you it wouldn't blow out. To monitor this, you can simply put your hand in front of your mouth and feel how much air is released. This is great to strengthen breath control for long phrases. Practice these exercises often. Record your progress in your journal. Try to take breaks at stop lights when you drive or every fifteen minutes during the day to breathe fully and freely.

Body alignment is important in vocal work. Yoga can be a wonderful tool for breathing and good posture, if it is taught correctly. I studied dance as part of my acting regimen. The problem with dance is that it can promote shallow breathing. Effective vocal work is all about using strong breath support to create sound from a relaxed and properly placed instrument.

Think of yourself as a building with each vertebra stacked solidly upon each other. My osteopathic physician, Virginia Johnson, D.O., says that most people usually have twenty-four bones from the top of their tailbone to the base of their head. A simple slow roll up from a bent over position to standing gives you a sense of this. Slowly roll up and feel each vertebra stacking upon the one below it as you come up. The crown of the head is lifted. It's kind of like the old image of walking with a book on top of your head. Just do this for fun: Walk across the floor with a book on your head. Keep your eyes focused at eye level with your chin parallel to the floor. Now resume your normal body stance. How is it different?

Sitting requires good alignment—and may be more challenging. Unfortunately, computer work can be very detrimental with bad ergonomics. For example, if the screen is not at eye level we may move our head down or up to compensate and develop neck tension. Therefore, it's important to have the screen, keyboard, and mouse placed correctly to do the least amount of harm to our bodies. Driving can be another pitfall for posture. Dr. Johnson gave me a great image for sitting. She said to think of the pelvis in a three-dimensional sense because it's shaped like a bowl. Then imagine your pelvis as a four-footed bowl with each foot equally placed. You need to be centered on your hips, not leaning too far forward or back, otherwise the airflow may be hampered. Refer to the article, "Sitting At Your Computer" at *www.coreawareness.com* for more information.

Dr. Johnson says that as you take in air you're filling a vacuum space in the body. In order to maximize your intake of air, you need to allow your body to expand freely. If you think of the flexibility of a bellow, you'll get the idea. For example, you should feel your lower back, abdomen, and ribs expand freely. *As you let your pelvic diaphragm drop, you can move more freely.* Proper alignment and breathing help to maximize airflow through the body. In contrast, if you are hunched over or not properly centered, you may restrict your breathing.

Proper alignment, strength, and relaxation are required to fuel the breath. This takes time to master and to unlock improper postural patterns. As I mentioned earlier, Pilates is an excellent way to organize the body. Pilates is a systematic series of exercises that helps to strengthen the abdominal core to create efficient body movement. My Pilates instructor, Adrienne Dalsemer, adds, "The very foundation of core strengthening begins with proper breathing."

Some people swear by the Alexander Technique. Virginia Griffith Frank, PT, Certified Teacher of the Alexander Technique, says: "The Alexander Technique is an intelligent way to solve common movement problems by training a person to notice their movement, release compression and move with ease and expansion. This skill will help prevent injuries and enhance performance. It is also a re-education in learning how to use your body appropriately during the course of your daily activities. The result is the reduction of stresses on bones, joints, and internal organs."

Everybody is different so you must experiment to find out what works best for you. You will know if something works if it enhances the power of your breath and sound.

Before you start to work, take this quiz to help you discover your postural patterns.

BODY/BREATHING QUIZ	T	F
I sit for hours at the computer without taking breaks.		
I can stand on one foot easily, on each side.		
I keep my eyes at eye level when I walk.		
I stretch regularly.		
I know when my body is off center.		
I hold my breath often when I'm stressed.		
I clench my teeth.		
When I gently rub my jaw hinge it's tight.		

After completing this quiz, be aware of the areas you need to modify. Take breaks from repetitive stress activities and breathe fully in those breaks. Know where you hold tension and concentrate on releasing it. When you approach vocal work, be grounded in your feet or sits bones. Take air up and make sure to expand your back as you breathe. Also, be sure to keep your shoulders down.

Exercise Your Imagination, Not Your Voice

As you begin to work, you must take good care of your instrument. You never want to stress the voice by excessive workouts. Use good judgment and work in short stints as you pick up new skills. Build up to longer workouts slowly and take breaks often. Always just rest your voice between vocal work and relax while you are acquiring new characters. *If anything ever hurts, then stop doing it.*

Learn to use the *silent treatment* to preserve your voice. This basically means to focus on using your imagination and studying a script. Really break it down as a scene. Discover what you want and need. Imagine where you are and what you're doing. In other words, instead of reading it aloud, over and over, study it. Work out every angle before you speak. Save your voice. This becomes increasingly important as you approach documentaries, books, and animation.

If you ever do feel strained, rest the voice for as long as you can. Just don't talk. Also be careful when you speak on the phone. It's easy to pull your voice back and not use good breath support. Project your voice, don't pull back and rest on your cords. Of course, you don't want to yell into the phone but just integrate supported breath as you speak.

Strengthen Emotional Choices

Although excellent reading skills are needed for voice-over, you must never think of it as reading. Acting involves behavior and emotion and so does voice-over work. However, when you do voice acting, you will have to stand or sit in front of a mic and stay within its sound range. Therefore, if you do not want to sound *stiff*, you must turn your imagination to a *heightened level* and use minimal body language and facial gestures to trigger truthful work.

Joan Uttal Anderson taught me how to make strong acting connections in voice-over work. You draw on a repertory group of at least five of your real friends whom you imagine you're speaking to when preparing to read copy. You should select *one* appropriate friend that you imagine you're speaking to when you read copy. In order to make this real, you'll create a scene with a *who, what, and where.* Who are you? What are you doing? Where are you?

For example, if I'm doing a commercial for a new coffee, I might imagine I'm talking about it with my husband (*who*) while he's preparing the morning brew (*what*) in my kitchen (*where*).

On the other hand, I could have the conversation at a coffee shop (*where*) with my friend Shelly (*who*) as we decide what movie we're about to see (*what*).

First, you will pick at least five close friends to use as your imaginary scene partners for your home workouts. Remember to always focus on *only one* person when you read. Over time you will discover how different friends color your reads for different products. In the end, you'll create a more natural performance because you imagine you're talking to one real friend while having a conversation in a specific place.

If you think of the friend to whom you are speaking as a mirror that reflects back to you, then you can see how each friend gives a different tone to your read. It's like the mirror game in improv when you mimic your partner's movements exactly. You essentially take on their characteristics.

The style improv game is also a useful model to think of in voice-over. In this game, you might set up a simple scene of a couple going to the store to buy something. Then, you repeat the same scene adding different styles such as: horror, soap opera, and sitcom. You can think of your own simple acting as the core of the work you do. Then you simply layer a style on top of it; layering may help keep your acting choices truthful. You want the style to help you to become more alive and engaged, but you don't want the style to completely take over and make your acting one dimensional and artificial.

You also want to think about the type of character you will portray. Most commercials ask for a very easy conversational style. This uses who you are. You simply adjust your attitude to the scene and imagine you are talking to your friend. In this sense, you are closer to a "straight" character. On the other hand, if you were asked to portray a Lithuanian orthodontist with a lisp, this would edge toward "character" work (unless of course, you are a Lithuanian orthodontist with a lisp). Meg Ryan and Tom Hanks might sometimes be seen as lead straight actors. Paul Giamatti has played character roles, but he's also played the leading parts in movies, too. There is no reason an actor can't do both types of work.

Personal Workout—Movement Exercises

▶ You can't tap dance in the booth but you can choreograph moves outside the studio. Movement can help you find characters. Simply start with strong archetypes. Assume the pose of a wizard, a poor urchin, and a king or queen. Walk across the room. Play around with more types such as: the tyrant, the nerd, or the celebrity. Take a children's book and assume the body movements of all the characters. Do the same thing with your favorite book, play, or cartoon. This kind of practice can help you instantly create characters.

▶ Once you've played around with full out movements, reduce the activity to simple stances you can use standing at a mic. In other words, find minimal body language and facial gestures to help you get into your character and free your voice.

▶ You can even get your creative juices flowing by doing a home version of the classic improv freeze tag game. First, you need to create a tape where you say "freeze" at least every 30 seconds apart. Play the tape and move expressively around the room. When you hear "freeze," hold your position in a pose and imagine you are starting a scene in that pose. For example, if I move around the room freely with a variety of movements, I might hear "freeze" when my finger is pointed out. I could use that pose to start a scene as a robber, or I could be pointing at something off in the distance. (Is it a star or a bear that escaped from the circus? Really make specific choices.)

▶ Imagine you're in a real scene with a real friend when you play this game and build different scenarios with a range of characters. Also make sure you're "out of your head" and just go with your first impulse so that you don't censor yourself. Make believe just like you did as a child! After all, no one is watching you here.

▶ Now bring it all down. Watch people at the mall or on the street and try to find their movements. Play around at home with the very real character types you see. Create the movement of the boss, the teacher, lawyer, nurse, racecar driver, etc. Now, record some lines from magazine ads as those characters. Play it back and see if you get a sense of the roles you're trying to portray.

▶ Tear out pages from magazine ads and keep them in a file. Pick an ad as you warm up to do your voice-over work and move like the character in the ad. In the end, use this muscle memory to help you create characters and minimize the body language at the mic for auditions and in the booth for jobs. Record some magazine copy with your new body language. Play back your work and listen to how your movement colors your reads.

▶ Don't forget to move freely in the hallway or restroom as you prepare for auditions at your agent's office.

Every actor has varying degrees of range and the same is true in voice-over. Some actors do real conversational parts, as well as broad animated characters that are different from their natural voice. They have a great vocal range. In contrast, some voice actors may have only one signature spokesperson sound. Your natural vocal qualities figure into what roles you play but you can always work at increasing your range. I will cover how to use dialects and various vocal placements to help increase your range, later in the book. As you progress through the forthcoming chapters, you'll move from straight roles to broad characters. For example, many documentaries require your natural sound but you'll build broader characters for animation.

Defining the Boundaries—Approaching Copy

First, let me clarify what I mean by copy. It is a script used in advertising. When you work at home you can use magazine advertising copy. It may be difficult to read because it's not always written for the spoken word. Raising your bar higher is always the goal in the home workout. For instance, practice reading articles from the *New York Times* or the *Wall Street Journal* to one of your imagined friends for at least five minutes, five times a week. If you can't find these newspapers, use something equally dense that will raise the bar of your reading skills. Get creative; choose anything dense to improve your cold reading skills.

In essence, when you read, you are translating something from the written word to the spoken word. Therefore, feel free to pencil in notes that may help you make something sound like speech. This includes throwing away written punctuation and redefining it to make it sound more conversational. Improvise the lines in your own natural words as if you're talking to a friend to get a feel of the flow for pauses and connections. Try to listen to conversations in everyday life and mimic an authentic flow of speech in your workouts.

When you're starting out, you need to work on cold reading skills and the ability to analyze copy and deliver it like you're having a conversation with someone. It's important to read word for word and not take your eyes off the page (however, it should not sound like you're reading word for word). You should not skip ahead because you'll make a mistake. You must always record your work and really listen to it.

Finally, always make this a dialogue and never a monologue. You are having a conversation with someone you really know. Therefore, you have to imagine what they are saying to prompt you to speak. Write out their lines and even do *their part* and then do yours. No one wants to hear you read.

They want to hear you speak to them. For example, the script reads as follows: *Bread . . . it's not just for sandwiches.*

Here's how you could make it a dialogue:

FRIEND: "What are you eating?"

YOU SAY: "Bread."

FRIEND: "But I thought you only used it for sandwiches."

YOU SAY: "It's not just for sandwiches."

Make all your choices fun, appropriate, and important. You have to believe everything you've devised so you drag us out of our humdrum life. All great art takes us away—so be creative. Imagine a scene that can justify why you are there. What just happened—you got a flat tire, went into the gas station for help, and lo and behold, you bought a winning lottery ticket. Always come from somewhere; then you can really go places.

Play the Game

That's all you have to do. If you engage your total concentration you'll entice the audience to listen—the reason we're fascinated with Meryl Streep is because she has focus and concentration on her character. She's really caught up in her given scenario. Focus and concentration take practice but things like meditation, juggling, and tai chi can help improve your skills.

You are a sound production machine or instrument. Think of yourself and treat yourself as a beautiful violin or piano. You'll perform like one. Treat yourself poorly and you'll perform poorly.

If the mic frightens you, you need to make an adjustment. As my acting coach Bob Luke used to say about the camera, "it's an inanimate object!" Therefore imagine the mic is one of your best friends. You'll be more believable and you just might get an agent to listen to you. Endow the mic with great qualities. No agent is going to do more for you than the mic. The microphone is your best friend.

Speaking of agents, I can hear you across the winds asking, "How do I get an agent?" My answer is to focus on the work and the agent will come. I'll discuss agents in greater detail later in the book. Don't worry. If you know you can do this and you have talent, you'll get an agent. Put all your energy in performing and other people will want to hire you. Focus on friends—people who support you and give you breaks early on in your career are crucial.

In the end, if you love to perform at the mic and read out loud religiously, you will be hired at the right time in your career. No one walks out the door one day and decides they will play at Carnegie Hall that night. Foul shots aren't made by accident with two seconds left in a game. It takes consistent practice to swish those shots. You can't nail an audition or impress clients without the same tenacity.

Before you begin your home voice-over work, you should warm up first.

Key Suggestions

- Always listen to your home workouts objectively (note your improvements).

- Practice audition techniques. You'll only record one or two takes so you need to perfect focus and relaxation skills. Also, rehearse the piece prior to recording just as you would at an audition.

- Be patient.

- Practice reading aloud a lot. You are not coming to a class so I suggest you work for about twenty to thirty minutes, five times a week (minimum).

- You should never strain. Always drink plenty of room temperature water throughout your vocal work.

- Always imagine you are speaking to one real person in a real scene.

Warm Ups

(Refer to the audio CD to hear these exercises)

1 Take a shallow breath and say your name. You'll discover this isn't right.

2 Lie on your back with knees bent. Breathe in and out ten times.

3 Take that breath support and release an *s* sound. Practice every day and see how long you can release the *s* sound.

4 Hum a simple tune. Try to place the sound behind your front teeth.

5 Sing some tongue twisters to simple songs. (*Refer to the tongue twisters in the appendix.*)

6 Gently massage your jaw hinge area (no harsh pushing—just be aware of tension and try to relax it with focus and concentration.)

7 Yawn gently to open up your palate area.

8 Do a siren on an *e* from your lowest note to your highest note.

9 Stick your tongue out and bring it back in five times. Next, wag the tongue from side to side.

10 If you're a singer, you'll know how to trill your tongue on a scale or make a motorboat kind of sound on a small scale up and down.

11 Stick your tongue out softly and gently between the teeth, then barely bite it and say, "a, b, c" holding it out. Do this three times. Then do the same but say, "one, two, three." Now, find something to read, and then do the exercise and read the passage.

12 Say an *mmm* sound like a hum and then say a few words in that same *place*.

Turn Up Your Imagination

You're always a person in a place with a purpose. Always give yourself breather breaks where you take deep breaths and relax or just laugh as long as you can to release tension.

It is important to keep your focus on the page at all times. If you act, you'll want to look up because that's how you're used to working, but you can't do this in voice-over while you're learning the technique. The focus is on the page. Even if you imagine seeing your friend's face as you read you must put your focus on the page. Think of it as a marriage of the imagination and reading in one place—the page. Your mind sees your friend and the words.

When you become more advanced, you'll learn to juggle the voice to picture technique. I'll go into that in greater detail in chapter 6. However, in the beginning learn to stick with the words. Use your imagination to enhance your sense memories. Hear things, see things, smell things, taste things, and touch things with your imagination, as you read.

Commercials have tonal nuances much like the broader placement and pitch variations in animation. Really listen to different types of commercials to discern the different tones. Hear the bright reads for supermarkets or the smoother, often breathy sound of car commercials. Catalog the tonal placements for as many commercial types as you can. Laundry detergent commercials, for example, have a different vocal tone than medical products. This detective work will help you understand the subtle differences between products on the market.

Personal Training Workout

▶ Listen to one-half hour of TV and radio commercials. Use the voice-over style list in the appendix and notice what kinds of voice-over styles are in the spots you hear. In a journal, note what you like and what kind of spots you can do professionally.

▶ Practice your voice-over skills. Create a repertory group of at least five real friends you know. Imagine you're speaking to one of your real friends when you work on copy. Work on building a strong connection to a single real friend when you perform. Always create a dialogue when you work by imagining what your friend says that prompts you to speak. Record some magazine ad copy using these techniques and really listen back. Evaluate how realistic you sound.

▶ Use your audio recorder to record commercials on television and the radio. Listen to the spots and try to get a sense of national and local commercials. Hear the differences. Transcribe them and practice the copy to get a sense of different types of campaigns. Listen to your work to make sure you've captured the nuances of each style.

▶ Practice reading the newspaper and magazine ads to different friends whom you imagine you're talking to just like in everyday life (ten minutes a day for five days). Also practice tongue twisters. If you don't practice, explain the reason why in your journal.

▶ *Note: when you record, try to do it like a performance.* In other words, read it all the way through once. In an audition, you may get direction and do a second take, but you'll have to self-direct your second take in your home workout.

▶ Take a piece of commercial copy. Play around with reading it as if it were a car commercial, pet product, floor wax, or phone company. It may help to think of a specific friend for each product. This is also a good way to break stale patterns you may have when you approach copy. Listen back and see if your choices match your reads.

▶ *Smile when you read copy.* See how that instantly warms it up. Now add brightness or earnest sympathy to the smile. As Uta Hagen suggested, there are many ways to cry. Find as many different smiles as you can with the same copy. There's a sarcastic smile, for example. Have fun and catalog your observations in your journal as you listen to your recordings.

▶ Really work on your sense memory skills as you read. Take one script. Imagine seeing a friend's face as you read through it. Then imagine seeing the place where your scene occurs. Switch to hearing your imagined scene partner's voice in between lines. Imagine senses that might be appropriate to the scene. Listen back and notice if you made strong connections as you read.

················

Key Web Sites: Voice-over and Agency database – *www.Voicebank.net*

Care of the Voice—*www.Choirsinger.com*

Tongue Twisters—see the Web link and my tongue twisters in the appendix

My Favorite Voice-Over Artists: Don LaFontaine and Sally Kellerman

(Go to house reels on Voicebank.net—you don't need a password).

················

3

Getting Ready to Compete

*Y*ou can really do a lot on your own. It takes discipline but if you put your mind to it you can do it. The *who, what,* and *where* take place in all scenes. You can practice breaking down these elements by using ads in magazines or scripts on Web sites like *www.Lacasting.com* or *www.Showfax.com* (fees may incur). Use these scripts or magazine advertising copy to play around with creating different set-ups.

For example, if you refer to the Alamo Script from A&E in the appendix on page 125, you can see how this works. First, do it as if you are a teacher (*who*) talking with a student about history (*what*) in a classroom (*where*). Now make an adjustment and just make your best friend the student to make it more conversational and easy. Next time, imagine you are a reporter talking to your best friend (*who*) about a news scoop (*what*) at a news conference in the Beverly Hills Hotel (*where*). The possibilities are endless. It's important to listen back to takes to see how your choices shape your reads. Try to imagine you're speaking to real friends in the scenes to keep your reads authentic.

Use your journal and note how detailed you can make your scenarios. The more detailed your choices, the better. See yourself in the place in your mind's eye before you read. See five specific things in the room. Imagine what you are wearing for different roles.

We always come from somewhere and go somewhere in life. Therefore, all scenes are read as if something just happened. For example, if I just won the lottery before I answer the phone I'm probably going to be upbeat and excited. In contrast, if I just got a ticket on my car then when I answer the phone I may be irritable. In theatre, this is like the preparation you do to go on stage. Let's say you're coming on stage to proclaim that your house has been robbed; you've got to imagine seeing the destruction before you come on stage to say your line. This is a wonderful tool in voice-over because you can't start cold when you read copy. Instead, you imagine what kind of scene happens prior to saying your scripted line. Therefore, you're reacting to something real and important.

For example say the line, "Honey, get the door, it's the plumber," with different set ups, such as: after a car just crashed into your home, a bill collector just called you on the phone, you just won a thousand dollars, etc.

Music is a great way to add tone and mood. I used music as a shorthand to give my voice actors direction when I was a promo writer/producer. It was the fastest way to communicate mood, rhythm, and tone.

For example, look at the HBO Boxing script in the appendix on page 137. What kind of music would work—fast-paced action, classical, or rock? As a producer, I would listen to stock music selections and read the copy. Any of the above might work but a fast-paced action piece would add more energy to the spot and the voice-over read. To understand this, think of the kind of music that is used for an action adventure movie or a network sports feature. These music selections add intensity to the scenes. Rock and classical music flow with the motion but don't add that extra edge of a typical action adventure style of music. Use music as a tool to play with your script. Try to imagine what kind of music would be used in the final spot.

Always have fun. Enjoying stepping outside your life into an imagined scene is the key to making voice-over believable. Don't forget to put energy in your body to add more realistic touches to the scene! One of the ways to recreate believable moments is to substitute something from your life in the scene. You use a substitution or "as if " situation in your own life to personalize something in a scene. For example, if you are recording a spot for a lottery, you can substitute feelings you had when you won something in the past. When I performed the live-event voice-over for *Nicole Kidman, An American Cinematheque Tribute*, I imagined that it was *as if* my character was a veteran star who had to save the award show. I substituted my feelings from walking elbow to elbow with celebrities when my husband won a primetime Emmy award, with my real life role as a live spokesperson at a show filled with Hollywood stars. You just have to find substitutions in your life that are a good match for the copy.

Use Your Hands to Free Your Voice

You need to let your hands move freely to loosen up and add emotion to the voice. Make sure your shoulders are relaxed and your scapula is down. Now play around using your hands and fingers freely to help express what you're saying. Experiment with puppets to add a fun twist. Imagine that the puppets help you communicate your ideas. Put your energy into letting them express movement and emotions. Keep your eyes on the page. The idea here is to have fun and be free!

Record your voice both using your hands and not using them. Do it silently just using your hands and then read it. You'll usually notice more life in your reads when you use your hands. Keep practicing this all the time until it comes naturally when you read at the mic.

Act scenes out silently so you don't get stiff or stuck. Play all the parts full on. In other words, improv a whole scene, then perform the copy. This adds color and life, which is essential in keeping a listener involved. Smile between takes or laugh to stay relaxed.

Old radio plays and current ones have a lot of energy. You have to think about that when you approach voice-over. Listen to Guy Noire on *Prairie Home Companion* for a contemporary example. If you want to explore radio from the past on the Internet, check out *The Shadow* and *The Burns and Allen* show. Go to *www.Old-time.com* for a trip down memory lane.

You're creating a whole world when you step up to the mic that is as exciting as those old plays and shows.

Personal Training Workout

▶ Collect your old magazines. Randomly select pages of ads for the *who, what,* and *where* of your copy. Even if it doesn't fit, read a piece of copy with different set-ups. Listen to your voice recordings and see if you've created new and interesting acting moments.

▶ *Learn to create your scene with what just happened or the moment before.* Give yourself four lines that you say out loud to your friend, whom you imagine you're speaking to, and then do your part. Listen back and see if your choices were believable.

- Practice copy with three different instrumental pieces of music like rock, jazz, and classical. See how music is a powerful tool to draw on when reading copy to create style and mood. Listen to your recordings and make sure you let the music influence your reads.

- *Use voice-over copy to practice.* You can start practicing audition techniques for fun. Take one piece of copy and prepare to perform it like you would at an audition. First you'll say or "slate" your name, then you'll state the product and slate number. For example, I'd say "Janet Wilcox, HBO take one." Then just record the spot two times. The object of this exercise is to improve your focus. However, don't make your performance pushed or fake. Imagine you've only got a limited time to say something important to your friend. Let a real energy and conversational style help create a truthful performance.

- In a class, you read in front of a group, and in a professional setting, you'll read for a casting director or agent. Try to find someone you can use as an *audience* to listen to you as you perform from time to time. But remember you are not reading to them, you are always having a conversation with a real friend you imagine you're speaking to when you perform. You are just reading for a friend or spouse to get used to performing in front of someone.

- *Practice legal disclaimer copy with a stopwatch at home.* Turn to page 121 and look at the sample legal disclaimer copy. The timing for the read is indicated in the parenthesis at the end. That is the number of seconds you have to read the copy. Practice by starting the stopwatch then reading and stopping it at the end. Keep the read connected to an acting choice to improve your articulation and create a truthful performance.

Key Web Sites: *www.Lacasting.com* and *www.Showfax*
for sample scripts

My Favorite Voice-Over Artists: Chris Murney and Vic Caroli

Learning the Rules of Radio and TV

You need as much energy and presence to deliver one line as you do to perform a fully scripted sixty-second spot. Radio and TV spots have a different feel. When we listen to the radio, it brings pictures to our minds—radio is an aural medium, and the sound has to create the entire scene. Radio scripts have multi-character scenes, straight talk throughout, or voice-over and sound bites. Really listen to the radio this week and notice how different it is from TV. A lot of radio spots require multiple voices, so they can be financially rewarding to more voice actors (because television spots usually only have one voice unless the tag at the end is done by a different performer).

Television voice-over complements the visuals whether it is graphics or live action. It's like a marriage of voice and picture. Therefore, it's important for you to always read storyboards or have strong images in your mind when you do voice-over for television. Watch and listen this week to television commercials. TV spots may have very few words in the script. Notice how different voice-over styles complement advertising campaigns.

All of these observations will help you when you approach copy. You should always determine if a spot is for TV or radio so you can *set the stage* properly for your work.

If you have time to transcribe current spots and practice them, this will help you reinforce these ideas. Even though you've seen the spot, you'll · still have to interpret the work and bring your unique choices to the copy.

Exercise being a producer—take a TV script and sketch a storyboard or list the visuals. Then think about the music and sound effects. Take a radio spot and list the sounds. Really use your imagination—you are the producer. It's your spot. Let the sounds come alive in your mind as you create your radio spot. Close your eyes and see and hear your television script.

If you learn to think like a producer and writer, then you will get a sense of the vision or creative direction for the spot. As a voice-over artist, you need to fulfill this vision and make it come to life. You should never just see words on a page. Give yourself strong colorful images and sounds to help play out your scene. You are a character in an environment. Make it one that will entice an audience.

Personal Training Workout

▶ In your journal, note at least five differences between radio and television copy. Really sit down and listen to thirty minutes of radio spots. Then watch TV spots. Record some spots on tape. While recording, turn down the sound on your TV. Play the videotape and create and record your own voice-over for a spot. Play back the audio and listen to your improv. Next, play back the video and listen to the actual commercial voice-over. The point here is to get a sense of how voice-overs work with pictures.

▶ Now see different styles. Do some channel surfing and get a sense of the different ways voice-over helps create the tone of a piece. In your journal, note the different vocal styles.

▶ Take a piece of copy and prepare to read it. Then turn it over and improvise it. Simply talk to your friend about it. By doing this, you're creating the essence of it. You'll see how well you are connected to the subtext and acting of the copy. The subtext is the emotional truth beneath the words. For example, I can say, "That's fine honey," and really mean "I'm mad as hell that you're not listening to me." In other words, our real feelings and the way we behave can exist beneath the words. The best way to experience this is to observe people and listen for what's really going on between people in everyday scenes. You'll also find subtle clues in the body language people exhibit.

▶ Now just try to improvise some copy and don't worry about what you say—this is not word for word. Try to add this spontaneity to all your work. Always put copy in your own words to personalize it while you rehearse. Play back your tape. How would you grade your creativity?

▶ Today, advertisers want you to sound conversational. They want you to sound just like you do hanging out with your friends or whatever the scene dictates. Aside from using acting to make a scene real, you need to know how you talk. *Leave a tape recorder on long enough that you'll ignore it and record your voice.* Listen back.

Compare that to your home voice-over workout recordings. Are you sounding like you're reading or talking?

▶ Do a substitution exercise. Read a script as if you were talking about the same thing you discussed when you recorded your real conversation. Create other substitutions. Do the script as if you're talking about your cat or husband or job. Improv real conversations in between your work with the scripts. Listen back and notice how the choices changed the nuances of your reads.

▶ *Perform practice copy as if you are doing an audition.* Practice reading Web addresses at home. Work on phrasing and marking copy in a way that helps you prepare for pauses, long phrases, and any road-blocks you may encounter. Practice working on both raw and marked-up copy and see what works best for you. *You will need to master both techniques in voice-over.*

· · · · · · · · · · · · · · ·

My Favorite Voice-Over Artists: Marcus Lovett and John Matthew

· · · · · · · · · · · · · · ·

Play Book

Breaking down a script need not be complicated or convoluted, but there are many approaches you can take.

You can first use the simple improv model of "Yes and . . ." to explore copy. When you create scenes in improv, you first learn to accept information and add to it, rather than denying it. Therefore, if my scene partner says, "You're fat," I say, "Yes, I've gained one hundred pounds and broke your chair today." Therefore, I don't stop the scene. I accept the situation that's established and embellish it with new information. Adding the *yes and* phrase, you can create a simple breakdown for copy. You're always adding information to the first thought; you're building a case.

Taking an improv model let's just use the *yes and* phrase as a guide with the Bensens' script in the appendix. After you read the first line, say "*Yes and* I feel guilty but I'm not sharing it." Adding the "*Yes and* . . ." phrase helps you make connections in the copy so that it flows as one piece. You're also supporting what the character really believes. His inner thoughts are something like: "I love this burger and I've got enough money to treat my friend on a tight budget!" The marketing message that is conveyed through the copy is "the consumer gets value and quality."

The most important thing to think about in the above line, however, is the buck. It's mentioned three times. *Every spot has a sole purpose to differentiate the product from others just like it.* Listen to the slogans about products, those one-line sentences that make a statement. In this case it might be, *"Bensens' has the best burger for a buck."*

Always think about opposites when approaching copy, too. Turn it around. What if Bensens' was overpriced and awful? You'd be angry. You'd be disappointed. If you read copy for a car that is fuel efficient, imagine having a car that is a gas-guzzler. In other words, see the ways your product relieves you from suffering from the loss of money, love, or poor health.

Look at Copy from Every Angle

Commercial copy often uses comparisons to make a point. For example, "I couldn't get my clothes clean with *Sudso*. I washed and re-washed them but then I switched to *Cleano* and they were brighter than ever!" Comparisons may also be used to illustrate how unhappy we are when we don't have the one thing our product can deliver. Nobody likes dirty clothes; when they're clean we have confidence.

With this idea in mind, break down a script based on emotions. Using the Bensens' script we've got: (1) bliss, (2) guilt, (3) greed, (4) pride, (5) generosity, (6) happiness, and (7) confidence. By doing this you'll create more levels to your read. Break it down just like you would divide acting scripts into *beats* (i.e., different thoughts).

Another thing that is important in breaking down the script is to determine what kind of character you are portraying. Who is our Bensens' dude? Language is an important key because it reflects social class. Who says the word *buck*? Is this guy a big spender? Let's see: he feels he can splurge on two dollars. He feels rich spending three dollars by the end of the script. Compare this to an ad for a high priced car or HDTV.

Another thing you need to do is really identify with the product. Paul Sills illustrated this by explaining that sometimes when we watch a baby, we totally mimic it and become engaged—all of a sudden we're saying silly words and becoming one with the baby. In the same way, we have to engage our full attention on why we need the product. Let's say we have stains on our clothes. All we can think about are those awful stains on our shirt and how much we want to get rid of them. Finding the solution to our problem becomes an obsession. We almost become the stain. Commercial products provide the perfect antidote to our problems.

Do a free association with the product. Write or say things that pop into your head. Even if it doesn't make sense, play with it. Always look for the location and situation of the scene. In this case, it's at the Bensens' restaurant. If the commercial copy you have doesn't have a defined place, then you must devise one. Record different choices for a variety of places for your copy and see which one works best when you listen to your work.

Finally, you are a consumer when you give in to the reality of the script. You both reflect and lure like-minded consumers to buy the product. Using the Bensens' script, you're someone who doesn't have a lot to spend and when you do, you want quality.

Add more color to your character. What do you wear? Is it jeans and a tee shirt or a tux? I think we know it's the former. Keep adding to the details. Are you married? What kind of lover do you like? Is your home big or small? Where did you go to school? The choices are endless; the point is to develop a list of features for your character you can fill in on the spot. It might be as basic as:

- Age

- Job

- Marital status

- Hair product you use

- Favorite sport

Play around with your home workout so your imagination will be full when you're under the gun at an audition. *Also give your character a name.* This really helps to anchor your work. When I learned this from voice actress and coach Pamela Lewis, it was very liberating and helped me see that every voice-over character is equally invested with emotions and needs. The genre style just helps to shape the world the character inhabits.

Remember, ads lure us because they have something so cool we want it. We need it so badly that we're going to buy it as soon as possible. This is shamefully obvious in the infomercial mantra—"But wait—there's more!!!" As the infomercial keeps adding on benefits, we want the product even more. We feel we can't live without it. We're also enticed by the "limited time offer." We don't want to lose out on the offer so we act quickly. It's all about raising the stakes. Your character's wants and needs

Promo Copy

Russia: Land of The Tsars
The Word Everyone Feared
:30

VIDEO	AUDIO
	A world premiere event...
	In a bold and reckless nation the one word
	everyone feared.
	TSAR
	Ivan... Peter... Catherine... and Nicholas
	This Memorial day feel what life was like under the most
	treacherous rulers in the world.
	Russia Land of the Tsars begins Monday May 26th at 9pm
	only on The History Channel.
	A story so incredible... it can only be true.

should be as compelling as those of the consumer mesmerized by the infomercial. This also gets back to the old acting question—who am I? What do I want and when do I need it? Chances are, with commercials you needed it yesterday.

I alternate between using circles and underlines so I can distinguish words that are close together. For example, in the first line, "world" is circled because it's important, while "premiere" is underlined to set the thoughts apart. It also signals that the word "world" is special in a different way. The fact that the show opens globally adds a special allure and excitement to the premiere.

In the second line, I've used a squiggly line under "reckless" to indicate the line implies shakiness and imbalance. "One word" is underlined to create a single thought from two words. This speeds up the rhythm to create more excitement. "Tsar" is underlined to add a dramatic feel.

Personal Training Workout

▶ When you breathe will affect the flow and interpretation of your read, just as phrasing shapes the meaning of the lyrics in a song. Find out how your breathing can change the flow of your work. Try marking copy where you think you *should* breathe. Also, learn to breathe spontaneously just like you do in everyday life. Both methods are important to practice. If you read a book, you can't always mark every breath. However, in advertising copy, a client may want it read with a specific breathing pattern. Listen for your breathing in your recordings to hear if it's natural. Observe what sounds false in your journal.

▶ You should also play with marking copy to help create signposts for your performance, and reading without marking copy. There's a detailed breakdown of ways to mark copy in James R. Alburger's voice-over book *The Art of Voice Acting.* You can see an example of how I mark my scripts below.

Every name listed from "Ivan" to "Nicholas" has a line behind it to denote an even down-inflection. In other words, when I read each name, my voice shouldn't go up.

The title, days, and times are marked to make sure the viewer knows when to watch. Please note that *only* and *exclusive* are always significant because they signal that a show is available on no other network.

If you mark copy, please be aware of over-emphasizing words in an unnatural manner when you perform. *Use the following home workout checklist when you listen to your recordings.*

HOME WORKOUT CHECKLIST	T	F
My performances sound like my natural speech:		
I believe I'm having a conversation with a real person:		
I don't emphasize or hit words in an unnatural fashion (really listen for this):		
When I breathe it sounds natural and justified:		
I'm creating a scene that is believable:		

The Tryouts—Auditions and Casting

I killed at the audition but wasn't the right type. That's the actor's moan on many a day. Every commercial needs a specific type of voice to fill the part. It's often not the actor's fault; it's just how the numbers add up.

Casting, especially in commercials, is a numbers game. You have to audition enough to hit it lucky and be perfect for a part. Ads have very specific visions to capture audiences. Actors and voice-over talent must fit into this very unique style.

How does it all happen? First a business needs to tell the public about its product. The advertising agency executive will find out what the client needs to say about a product and tell the ad-agency creative team the objectives. Then the creative director works with the art director (the visionary) and the copywriter. Together they come up with a brilliant campaign and scripts. The producer then gets involved with production while a casting director is hired to find the talent, or agents are contacted directly.

A casting director will call agents and request talent for the auditions. Perhaps they've heard someone they like and will call that person based

Personal Training Workout

▶ Start listening to professional demo reels on Voicebank to get a feel for your competition and what you'll need to do to create your own reel. If you can't do that, watch TV spots and listen to radio commercials.

▶ Pick out five pictures of people from magazines. Say some of the copy lines as if you are these *types*. Notice how you use pitch for each character. Practice reading magazine copy, working on your own unique natural style, five days a week for fifteen minutes. Do you sound like a real person, or is it forced?

▶ *Define your career goals.* Start to think of five people that you know who can help you find work, get an agent, or record copy. Come up with networking tools to meet new people. Use the *bull's-eye* approach to networking. Visualize a target. Place your most familiar contacts at the center and the least familiar ones on the outside. Work from the inside out when you start your search. Think about acting or improv classes that might help in the future. Write all your plans in your journal.

▶ *Prepare for your own home audition with copy that is a stretch for you. Give yourself five to fifteen minutes to prepare it and then record it. Listen back. Would you have booked the spot?*

▶ Take the *HBO Boxing copy* on page 137 and see if you can cast it from the talent on voicebank.net. Learn by example; listen to as many demos as you can in about a half-hour. What caught your ear? Were the actors dull, slow, *announcer-y*, and boring; or did they sound real, with vocal energy, and stop you in your tracks? Make a list of what makes you listen. Was there music or just voice? Use this to help create your own demo and to add to your performances.

▶ If you can't use Voicebank, watch TV and record breaks so you can listen to the talent. Now make a list of the candidates. Take a break and come back and cast your person for the spot. Try *casting* another spot. Decide how you would direct the talent. Perform and record the spot and then listen to it. Take a break, listen again, and record some more takes. Evaluate both sets of takes. Do you need more than two takes? Do you get stale on later takes or have energy?

▶ *Use your acting skills and imagine playing the part of an agent for a day. Break it down like you would if you were creating a character. What is a typical agent's day like? Do the same with a casting director or commercial producer and try to imagine what the writer does. In the end, understand what their wants and needs are, so you can fulfill them. The more you can take yourself out of the actor head the better.*

· · · · · · · · · · · · · ·

Key Web sites: *www.voicebank.net*

My Favorite Voice-Over Artists: Paul Christie, Wendy Dillon

· · · · · · · · · · · · · ·

on previous auditions. Next, the voice talent auditions with the script at the casting director or agent's office (or submits an MP3 audition). The client, creative team, and perhaps the director review the auditions and then narrow down their choices. Voice actors may or may not be brought back for *callbacks*. Finally, the talent is booked.

Keep in mind just the right voice is needed to bring a creative concept to life. You must give all you have to any audition. Often directors or ad executives remember your work and will call you in again. *Eventually you'll book the perfect job for you.*

Now you'll see how it all works. It's often not what you do at an audition but if you fit the part. Obviously, you should always try to fit the part. Work at understanding the creative objectives by being creative yourself. Be part of the creative team; try to see the big picture and the vision. *Have fun with the creative process and you'll always get hired.*

4

Finding Your Game

You never know what you can do well until you experiment with different voice-over styles. Sometimes you'll surprise yourself and uncover hidden talents or hit a roadblock on something you thought you'd do with ease.

Versatility can expand work options so there's no harm in practicing a range of styles. You never know when a fast-paced promo style will fold into commercial copy or the flexibility of animation skills will help you create characters for a book. So enjoy your journey through these different genres and don't hold back.

What's more, opportunities can arise quickly for jobs. The more tricks you have in your bag, the more likely you'll come home with cash. It's crucial, however, that you never hold back on a job or an audition even if you don't feel the genre is best suited for you. This is the reason you want to practice many different things at home. It gets you warm. Negative thoughts will stop you cold so don't ever censor your creative process in a professional setting.

In this chapter you'll learn about the different genres and explore acting techniques. You will then get a sense of professional auditioning and recording scenarios in chapter 6.

The One-Two Punch of Promos

What makes NBC different from HBO? Why should you watch *ER* instead of *CSI?* Strong promotion for networks and TV shows pulls you in to watch. It entices you and tells you when to tune into specific programs.

Today, each network makes its stamp with *branding* campaigns. It's sort of like how cattlemen would brand their breed to set them apart. Networks set their *product* (shows) and identity apart from the rest of the crowd.

Promos are hot. The voice-over talent must have strong energy to be heard over sound effects and match the intensity of the sound bites from the shows (but not pushed). Sometimes, spots have a lot of copy and your pace adds energy to it. Unfortunately, not all voice-over talent has that vocal punch for promos.

Think of how you love to talk about your favorite shows with your friends. It's no different with promos. You're sharing your excitement about a program with a real friend.

You'll need to study the different kinds of networks. For example, there's free network TV, basic cable, and pay cable. Some networks give broad programming choices while others offer selective entertainment. For example, HBO is a pay cable channel that offers a broad array of programs. On the other hand, The History Channel delivers programs dealing with a specific subject matter.

Now you need to really listen to the different stamps of all the networks to get a sense of their styles. *Listen and see where you fit in.* VH1 is radically different from CNN. Find five networks for you. Then you should select five specific shows from any network that you think you could promote.

Study every aspect of specific spots, from news promos to spots for shows to network IDs. Get a sense of every genre. Promo work is great because it is steady. If you are the voice of a network, you may be under contract. It's a great way to hone your craft and make a good living.

Watch each network and really listen to the pitch and pace of the spots. Don LaFontaine is a huge promo voice. Listen to him on Voicebank.

No matter what, try to stretch your talents. If you're excellent at doing comedy, then improve your drama skills. Promo sessions are very fast so you've got to have a full bag of tricks ready.

Timings are sometimes tighter in promos. You may have to pick up the pace. Practice your timing skill by using a stopwatch to time your work. Learn how to shave off seconds. You also may have to stretch for time as well. It's important to know how your internal clock works. When you transcribe spots always time them.

Going for the Gold with Commercials

A friend asks, "Hey, what have you got there?" "Oh, it's just the latest cell phone-computer-camera—and portable satellite," you reply. The fact is Americans love to buy things. *Commercialism is pounded into our souls from the crib.* First, it's toy commercials and then when we're adults, we graduate to all the fun high-tech gadgets the world has to offer.

If you doubt your consumer habits, keep a log of everything you buy. Just a trip to the supermarket alone yields a hefty score. Also, admit you love to share the news about your favorite items with your friends.

Well, this energy and enthusiasm is needed in your commercial voice-over work. Read commercials with lots of energy and attitude. You've got to make the people you're talking with real and your scenes lively. Imagination must be full and free. Think about how you love to buy things.

On a serious note, you also will have more dramatic products like medicines, insurance, etc. You must be truthful. If the spot calls for drama, be real. Start coming up with a stockpile of situations in your life that were high drama with people you dearly loved.

Personal Training Workout

‣ Scan magazines, TV, and radio ads to get a sense of different character types needed for various campaigns. In your journal, note where you fit in best. Use the Web to research different companies and to get a feel for their advertising.

‣ List the products you buy and your top interests. For example, do you like cats and computers? Practice reading a range of copy you find. Listen back later and note in your journal which styles and products work for you.

‣ Pick five different faces from magazine ads, stand in the mirror, imitate the face then create the body posture that matches. Speak some of the copy in the voice you think matches the advertising campaign. Listen back and see if your style sounds credible. Practice commercial copy ten to fifteen minutes, five days a week. Add on pitch variations for a warm up. Sing copy from your lowest pitch to your highest pitch.

Key Web Sites: *www.Adweek.com* and *www.Wheresspot.com*

My Favorite Voice-Over Artists: Gene Hackman, Christine Lahti, Richard Dreyfuss, Jeff Goldblum, Stockard Channing, and Allison Janney.

The reason you want to have such a good time with commercials is that they can pay a good wage. Agents love them because they can bring fast money. With the *pay per play* on some spots, you'll make money every time the spot plays in different markets. Even with a spot rate you can make a nice fee for one day's work. (This of course applies to SAG and AFTRA rates and perhaps some non-union.)

The trick is to be patient. You may have to audition many times before you book a spot. Remember our casting exercise? Also, because every spot has a unique nuance you have to be just the right *type* to fulfill the artistic vision.

Therefore, the only way to approach this side of the business is to be playful. After all, you get paid to put yourself in an imaginary world. Make choices that inspire you so that you'll always be first on the casting director's list for future auditions. You can't focus on the competition, or if you'll book the job.

The 1,500-Meter Race: Long-Form Scripts

Often documentary and industrial copy can be dry and therefore seduce a voice actor to do a narrator cliché. This trap can be avoided by building a strong character in a situation that warrants a conversation about the subject.

Another pitfall of the industrial can be length and language. Often it is quite difficult to read the words and perhaps the language may be complex. The only way to keep your head above water with this is to imagine you are an expert on the subject. It is very important that you say what you have to say to your friend.

Unlike commercials or promos, industrials and documentaries are often delivered with a more leisurely pace. You may be explaining how to do something new or telling a story. Either way, the listener has to take in the information slowly enough to comprehend it.

An offshoot of this is a marketing tape for a company. In this case, you are introducing new ideas to company personnel. This copy is more upbeat and energetic to excite employees to go out and promote the product. The pace will be determined by the style of the piece in this instance.

This type of work can be steady if you get a client who produces a series of tapes. You read more copy for a lower rate than for commercials, but it can be fun. It requires great acting skills to make dry copy sound conversational.

If you have an audition or booking for a product, go to the company Web site and download pages. Next, practice reading copy from the Web site. You'll get a sense of the language and can come up with some character choices too.

To make this more concrete, think of the narrator from the play *Our Town* by Thornton Wilder or the narration in the movie *Seabiscuit*. These people give the impression they belong in the story. They love to talk about the subject. Who might you be as the narrator for *Seabiscuit*? You might be a horse owner, or jockey, or sports reporter. Make a choice and then decide who you are talking to when you prepare industrial copy. Still, make it someone you know in real life, to keep it conversational.

All of the above applies to a show you narrate, too. You will want to keep your character consistent since you may read a script for a one- or two-hour program.

Personalize the Piece

Notice how different voice-over talent narrates everything from World War II documentaries to infomercials. The narrator adds tone to these types of reads. You've got to get a hook for yourself that makes the material accessible, real, and urgent to convey to someone.

Improvise a monologue for your character before you speak the lines. Create scenes leading up to the copy. Get strong visuals in your head to help illustrate what's going on. Close your eyes and see what is in the script as you rehearse. If appropriate, imagine the sound effects or music that may be used in the final product. For example, recently I was asked to record a job at home and the producer told me to think of classical music behind the piece. It was much easier to get a sense of the mood and tone for the read with this direction.

In the end, you need strong read aloud skills for an industrial or documentary session. You could narrate a one or two-hour program. You may be given changes in your session, so have a pencil handy. They may happen quickly. *Be ready to go with the flow. You may walk in to read copy nearly ice cold if there's been a heavy deadline.* You might be given a first draft to look at before the session, which can be helpful. If the copy is new, eyeball it a section at a time if you can't read it all through at once. Rehearse as much as you can and mark the copy.

Remember to breathe and know that this will take some time to perform. *Pace yourself so you have enough energy for the last takes.* You may want to sit rather than stand if it's a lot of copy. Remember to keep your alignment right. Drink sips of water so you don't get too dry.

Finally, let your character do the work for you. Hear it as a dialogue between you and your friend and just imagine your lead-in line. We explain things to people all the time and this is no different. You are explaining, telling stories, or describing something just as you do in real life situations.

Personal Workout

▶ Get a Sunday newspaper or magazine. Select an article and make character choices that are appropriate. Record the copy. Play it back and listen. *Now create offbeat character choices for your narrators and record and play back.* Devise high drama reasons why you have to say this copy. Really listen to your work and note in your journal if you need more energy or sharper characters.

▶ Get a technical manual from your car, VCR, phone, etc. *Make choices and read it.* Do it with accents in your rehearsal. Record yourself telling it to three different friends. Make three radically different choices for yourself and listen. Note in your journal if you can hear distinctive differences.

▶ *Remember you must sound like you are talking to someone.* Really make sure you reach this goal. Download information from various company Web sites. Select everything from medicine to space research topics. Raise your bar with different dense copy. Now really create a character that needs to say this information. Build a back-story for the character that makes it absolutely necessary to say this information. Listen and see if you feel the emotion behind the words.

▶ Have fun. *Pretend you are an expert on the subject.* You can again randomly pick subjects from magazines or use your copy as the subject. Do a one-minute improv monologue about your subject. Then read your copy. Listen and see if your character is credible.

▶ *Do improv monologues as a doctor, president, and biographer.* Then record and read copy as these characters. Listen back and evaluate your character work.

· · · · · · · · · · · · · ·

My Favorite Voice-Over Artists: Edward Herrmann, Alan Bleviss, Michael Carroll, and Michael McGlone.

· · · · · · · · · · · · · ·

Please slowly build up to long sessions. Don't just do thirty minutes of straight reading if you aren't used to it. Do this over time and take breaks and rest while you are building up your muscle.

The Marathon—Audio Books

Twenty-six miles is a long way to run. A runner must train many hours and build up to the race. Books are really the marathon of voice-over. Sessions may be several hours long and you're reading a great deal of material. In order to do this, you have to be a fine actor.

One of the traps of the book is the third person narrator. Just like with an industrial or documentary, an actor will assume a false tone. Again, narrating a book it is quite the opposite. You are in fact deeply invested in what you are saying. You need to say it—maybe as a confession or as a proclamation—with great emotion.

Every person, place, and thing has great significance to you. You know the people and you have opinions about them. Places bring images to your mind. You lived in this world. To do this you must decide who you are in this story. Are you a priest, housewife, or cop? How did the turn of events affect you? When you read the narrator's part, you must tell a story as if it happened to you; you are not just reading it.

Create a Believable World

You will bring different characters to life in the story. Create natural characters. These characters aren't usually as broad as many animated roles you'll play. You can portray some characters with an attitude and tone you use to imitate friends and family in everyday conversations.

When you start practicing reading books, you may find it easier to identify with a first person narrator. This narrator is more defined and you will have to fill in fewer details. Think about doing monologues. You can transfer a lot of those skills to a book reading. You're having a two-way dialogue with a friend even though it's not written that way. As with a monologue, create the lines that your friend says that prompt you to speak as you rehearse a book voice-over.

One of the biggest challenges of the book is keeping your characters straight. Therefore, it might be best to first focus on the narrator character when you do the exercises. You can then play around with the other characters too, but I'll give you more tools to help you create a broad array of roles in the forthcoming animation section.

For example, you'll practice talking back and forth between diverse characters. You'll also learn about dialects and vocal placements. Therefore, after you've done the animation exercises, integrate those techniques into your practice recordings of books.

I've structured the chapters this way so that you build up your reading skills with the long passages of books before you approach animation. This strengthens your reading skills, which is crucial to perform animated roles, because you literally have to read and act on the spot. After you've completed the animation section you should read the narrator and characters in succession from the children's books in the appendix.

The best way to understand this genre is to listen to audio books. You can go to the library and listen to them. Get a range of titles. Select things that interest you the most and the least. Even if it's a style you'll never do, you'll learn a lot from the pros.

Always listen to your own work and see if it is conversational and believable. It should always sound like you're talking to someone. You can go to the Web site for recorded books in New York, for guidelines on their auditions (*www.recordedbooks.com*). As with anything, reading for audio books takes practice too. It's good to record newspapers or books for the blind as a way to gain experience. Although these are most often volunteer jobs, they will prepare you for the fast-paced demands of narrating mainstream books on paid jobs. You need to build up to the long sessions necessary for competitive work. It takes strong focus and concentration to read long passages without making many mistakes. As with industrials, the pay is not on par with commercials; however, it's very enjoyable work if you want to pursue it.

Personal Training Workout

▶ Imagine you're telling a story about something to your friend. Record the story you tell. *Play it back and notice how emotional you were.*

▶ Prepare and record one page of a book. Use the emotions you had in your real life story in the previous exercise when you read the book. *Let the same feelings and passions drive you to speak.* Listen back. Did your real-life story help you bring it to life?

▶ Come up with more *as ifs* and substitutions for your book readings. (i.e., it's as if I'm talking about my friend dying of cancer). Write them in your journal.

▶ Substitute your feelings for a relative or friend under passages about similar characters. Use images of places that have strong meaning for you under the words. Listen back and figure out what choices are your best.

▶ Record yourself recounting the story from the page in your own words. Tell it to three different friends for different reasons. Then use this same energy underneath your reading of the page. Listen back. Does it sound real? Evaluate why something doesn't sound natural.

▶ *Come up with high stakes reasons for telling this story.* You're going to lose the family fortune if you don't tell it. Your child may die. Your lover will go off with someone else. Record different paragraphs with those choices and make strong connections. Listen and note if you hear the urgency.

▶ Practice a chapter using strong acting choices. See how much of it you can record without errors. *Change acting choices and see if that helps your reading abilities.* Practice consistently, build up your skills, and be very patient.

· · · · · · · · · · · · · · · ·

My Favorite Voice-Over Artists: Josh Hamilton reading Stephen King's *Riding the Bullet* and Paul Michael reading *The DaVinci Code*.

· · · · · · · · · · · · · · · ·

Relay Races—Multiple Character Radio Scripts

Shakespeare said, "All the world's a stage." Indeed, your homework is before you every day. You should be hungry to devour all those great real life scenes around you at the mall, doctor's office, or soccer game. It's important to observe these scenes because you may be called in to take part in slice of life scenes for radio spots. These can range from very realistic to broader character scenarios. You usually audition with another actor and read the parts together. Sometimes, I just record my lines for a home audition and imagine I'm responding to another character. Therefore, you must learn to imagine hearing your cue lines as well as responding to a scene partner's dialogue.

You need to study the relationships between people in everyday life to understand this work. In real life, we all play roles. I'm a mother, voice-over artist, wife, etc. Even though I am always myself, the "role" I play depends upon my relationship to the people with whom I am interacting. Always break down your script by role. In fact, take a script and do it three times, substituting different *roles* for the same part for fun.

Secondly, we all play status games in life. For a great explanation of how we all use status in real life, and in performance, see the "Status" chapter in Keith Johnstone's book *Impro.* Someone has high status and someone has low status. Think about that when you approach a scene. Also, play around with reverse status choices in a script when you rehearse. See what happens when the secretary or the maid or the garbage man is the high status character.

Where the scene takes place is very important, too. Our behavior is colored by where we are. We speak and behave differently in a church than we do at a basketball game. Now, first list the key points of each of those settings. Say it out loud if you like. When I did an improv show, I had to think fast. For example, a candy factory brings to mind a conveyor belt, *I Love Lucy,* being out of control, choking, etc. Turn the imagination up and you'll be more focused.

Then fill in your character. Refer to my character checklist in the appendix. What's your age? What's your vulnerability? Now add what you're doing to it. For example, *I'm buying a car for my sixteen-year-old daughter.*

You have your homework. Observe life. Figure out what's really going on with the people at the next table. (Let's see: she's having an affair and he doesn't know it.) Try to guess what the person does for a living just by observing how they move and talk.

Walk across the room and play five different roles you select from magazine ads. Now add status, next add character. Finally add the place. Finish the scene with what you're doing. Homework always involves physical workouts. You have to work on being an actor full out so when you go to the mic you can minimize the movements to help enhance your imagination.

Personal Training Workout

▶ Eavesdrop on three different scenes in real life. Observe the different types of people and their needs in the real-life scenes. Go home and imitate all the characters. Stand in front of the mirror and imitate their body postures. Walk across the room as the character you're going to play in your copy. Were you committed to your character?

▶ Watch sitcoms, soaps, and dramas to see how actors use their bodies, faces, and voices to emote. Watch half the show and then imitate the voices and body movements for half of the show. ★ *Note this is only to get you outside yourself to imitate, this is not acting. Acting comes from your unique and truthful choices in a scene.*

▶ Try an acting exercise where you improvise the dialogue of silent film actors with real truth and emotions. Practice both drama and comedy. Listen back and decide if you were truthful or faking it.

▶ Define status and real life roles of people you observe. Break down scripts with status and roles the characters play.

▶ *Practice a pretend phone conversation and record it.* Really listen and behave as you normally do. Connect to the listener and let their imaginary dialogue prompt you to speak. Then apply this to your voice-over work. Really build a dialogue with your friend before you say your first line. Listen back and see if you believe this was a real conversation.

▶ *Write your own multiple person script.* Refer to the appendix for one written by my former student, John Brosnan, on page 155.

▶ Play around performing both characters in sequence in the *Black Cow* script, on page 155, and record it. Then, just do your character and record it using your full imagination to make your lines sound justified, and grounded. Listen to your work after you have just recorded your lines; notice if you sounded like you were talking to someone.

Lost in Play—Crazy Animation

It's wacky, crazy, and goofy! Whatever you want to call it, it is never small or dull. Cartoon characters are big and full of energy. You need to use pitch, voice placement, and full out imagination to make these characters come to life.

You're liable to do at least two different voices in a union session and may do as many as three characters (or more if you are one of the stellar actors on *The Simpsons*). However, you'll want to build a large array of characters if you're serious about this kind of voice-over work. As stated before, take it slow and never strain.

Some characters are small. They may need more of a head voice like Mickey Mouse. Others are smart talking wise guys like Bugs Bunny. Space Ghost has that superhero voice that's over the top. Homer Simpson has a goofy kind of voice. Marge on *The Simpsons* has a crack in her voice, as do older characters like old grandma-types.

You must make choices in regard to placement; write logs to chart your progress on characters. Keep track of any troubles you encounter. For example, you may find a throat voice hurts. Make note of your easy and challenging characters.

You will learn all sorts of ways to flex your acting muscles in this chapter so that you build your range and create unique characters. However, when you work there is no time for fussing with your characters. You will have to use a quick improv model.

Bob Bergen: "What I do when auditioning, for every scene I always ask myself three questions: (1) Who am I talking to? (2) What is my relationship with them? (3) Geographically, where are they in the scene???

"How I decide these three questions allows for relationships to come through in the audition. If my character is talking one on one with another, I'll move into the mic as if it's the ear of the other character and just talk to them. If they are in a crowded restaurant, across the room, I give more volume to the read, etc. Most auditions don't give you all this info, so you the actor must make these choices."

Now you've got to learn to let go, too. You can't hold back. Have fun and turn down a cartoon sound track and dub in your own character voices. Then listen to the characters that are created. How did you do? Hear all different pitches and accents.

Dialects and vocal placement come in handy for animation. Remember they are merely technical skills to help create your characters. Learn about these tools in the next two sections.

The World Games—Accents and Dialects

"The rain in Spain," is the phrase Eliza Doolittle struggles with in the film *My Fair Lady*. The way we talk is a result of where we are raised and our social class. Actors need to develop a keen ear to discern the subtle sounds of a dialect.

It's important to really listen to everyone around you. I don't care if you're in a small town, you'll hear differences in speech patterns. Again, the world is your stage.

To pick up a new dialect, you need to listen and find out what key sounds are different. *Always use native speakers.* Listen, imitate the speech, and integrate it into your own mode of speaking. It's good to write down sounds phonetically so you really capture the unique patterns properly (if you don't know the IPA (International Phonetic Alphabet) write it so you will understand the pronunciation when you read it later).

There's also a natural rhythm and pitch variation to speech you need to feel. The southern accent can be slower. The British feels clipped with crisp consonants.

You can research dialects on the Web. Drama bookstores have recordings you can buy which break down the key phonetics for you. They also sell recordings of native speakers with authentic accents.

Any way you approach it, you must practice, listen, imitate, and integrate. Read the newspaper in your new dialect to make sure you have assimilated it and you're not just repeating what you've heard.

Watch TV shows or listen to radio programs with native speakers. You might pick up mannerisms and social patterns that will add color to your characters. (For example, watch BBC television programs.) If possible seek out native speakers in your area and eavesdrop as they speak.

If you feel awkward, be patient. It will come with practice. Before you know it, you'll be talking about the rain in Spain, too.

Personal Training Workout

▶ Learn to hear sounds all around you. *Perk up your ears and hear the sounds.* Imitate and use them.

▶ *Acquire a Southern and if possible a British accent.* Go to the Web link listed in the appendix to listen to authentic speakers. Watch TV shows, documentaries, and movies with authentic speakers. Review dialect CDs at a drama store or search the Web for dialect recordings you can purchase. Start to write a phonetic list of the sound patterns. Create body language to use at the mic. Imagine their home and social class.

▶ *Read the newspaper in your dialect.* Practice until you are comfortable with it. Then try it with copy and record it. Listen back and decide if you were true to the accent. Compare your work to authentic speakers and keep improving it.

▶ Practice a dialect diligently for a week. Do most of your home voice-over workout with it. The next week drop it and feel how light your workout is.

Key Web Sites: *www.idea.com* (see appendix)

My Favorite Voice-Over Artists: Doug Preis and Dan Castellaneta.

Going High or Low to Hit the Winning Mark—Voice Placement and Character

We place our voice in different ways to match our mood and you can feel the vibrations in different parts of your body. You can feel the top of your head vibrate for a heady voice like a fairy princess. In extreme cases, vocal placement creates a unique character. The heady voice is often used for supermarket spots—it's a bright voice; or think of a fairy princess or the blonde bombshell.

A *nasal voice* can be for a whiny type of a person. It can be a bit unpleasant and not appealing. Many times the *adenoidal voice* is used in cartoons (think *Boo-boo Bear*, for example).

A *throat voice* might reflect *The Godfather* or an old person. On the other hand, a *chest voice* resonates in our chest and it's quite full and can be sexy.

Take ten good breaths. Now just make a siren sound (like what you hear with an ambulance). Ride from your bottom to your top range with an *e* sound. *Easy—easy does it—never strain.* This is a wonderful exercise to work through your pitch range and get on top of your breath. It's also great to warm up so that you're not trying different vocal intonations ice cold. Now start listening to every person possible on TV. Imitate cartoon voices. Like with dialects, take the time to figure out where the sound is coming from. Is it more heady or nasal?

Work on one different pitch type each day for five days. Next, you can practice using these pitches for characters you create in a variety of scripts. On another week, tape a show and imitate small segments of one character each day of the week. This way you'll get a sense of how they express a full range of emotions.

It's important when you practice to really use your ear first rather than over stressing your voice. Always be careful not to overdo this exercise. Take breaks and drink water. Since you're a beginner, never use the voice to imitate more than five minutes straight a day when you're simply mimicking. Always take long breaks and drink water before doing other work. As stated before, this is not your own character work so you don't want to ever get vocal strain. This will take time to do so enjoy it.

Imitate celebrities. Mary Tyler Moore had that, "Oh, Mr. Grant," pitch. It's a great experience to imitate celebrities because it helps pull you into full character work. However, when you work you will make your own unique character choices. If you simply imitate others in your own work, you'll come off as a poor comparison. *You must always create your own new character that is organic to the scene.* The only exception to this is if you perfectly do dead-on impersonations.

Placement comes in handy with characters of different ages. Practice doing children's voices and imitate older people. Listen and see how many ages you can create.

Remember to create characters you can sustain (for as long as a four-hour voice-over session if necessary). Work on choices you can have fun with. Don't get locked into pitch. It's good to practice different ranges. Sing some of the copy from your lowest note to your highest note in your natural voice. Next, try and sing a simple tune in your character's voice.

Animation Acting

Animation requires excellent reading skills as well as acting and improv chops. In the beginning start slowly, then build more and more skills.

Study the Web pages of Daws Butler and Bob Bergen listed on page 177. Daws Butler created Huckleberry Hound and Bob Bergen currently does the voice of Porky Pig. The key here (and in all voice-over work) is to create very original characters and be fully committed to your work. Think of how the stutter of *Porky Pig* helped to define that character. Let go, take risks, and really add your most unusual touches to this work. Use a full range of vocal techniques.

Speaking of voices, don't forget to sing little songs for your characters. Use simple songs. Anyone can sing—really. First just try talking to the rhythm of the song if you feel uncomfortable matching a pitch. Elongate your vowels to the rhythm to give it a rounder, fuller sound like in opera. At the very least, you'll work on your rhythm and timing. Sing out in the shower where no one can judge you.

If you're afraid of taking singing lessons, don't be. I had a wonderful teacher at Ohio State get a tone-deaf person to match pitches. My singing teacher, Jill Edwards, in New York, is extremely patient and says that she has also worked with students like this in addition to her most advanced pupils.

There are technical tools that help you define animated characters. These include all the elements we've already discussed—pitch, placement, age, accent, body type, and archetypal characters (i.e. nerd or bully). You can assign a general energy for your character (such as laid back or uptight) and her strengths and vulnerabilities.

It's great to base your character on someone you really know personally as well as an existing cartoon character or celebrity. These things help you find your characters. However, these traits alone do not create heartfelt characters. Truthful acting does that, along with a playful and childlike imagination.

The Marriage of Acting and Improv

To lay good foundation skills, it might be useful to think of animation acting as the marriage of improv and theatrical acting. You need to be playful, be ready to respond quickly with broad character choices, and you need good listening skills. At the same time, you need very strong acting choices in the scene—much like the work you would do in breaking down a scene in a play. In the theatre you generally don't learn your lines until you find the

Personal Training Workout

▶ Record and evaluate all the vocal exercises listed below and analyze the credibility of your work.

▶ *Create the illusion of age by putting your voice in the right place.* Also learn how placement creates different character types.

▶ Use placement, tone, and character traits to bring your parts alive, even in everyday life spots. Make choices based on occupation and social status, too.

▶ Really listen to old people and children on TV and in real life. *Record copy as an old person and child.*

▶ Malls are a good source of a variety of people. Go home and create five different characters. You also can use accents.

▶ Children have so much energy and a unique variation of pitch and placement. Observe the vocal energy traits of as many different aged children as you can. See if you can imitate an array of children's voices. Record your various 'kids' and listen to see if they are believable.

▶ *Character comes through in the voice.* Again, listen to people around you, including friends and family members. Play around with different placements you hear. Imitate a nerd, snob, and bully and notice where the voice is placed.

▶ *Dub* voices on TV by turning the sound down and creating your voice work. Read comic strip characters.

· · · · · · · · · · · · · · · · ·

Key Web Sites: *www.comics.com*

My Favorite Voice-Over Artists: Michael Yurchak, Pat Fraley, Frank Welker.

· · · · · · · · · · · · · · · · ·

emotional truth under the lines. However, remember, this is just for you to use in your workouts to build your strength. You'll then have to draw on all your homework choices very fast using quick-sketch improvisation techniques for auditions and jobs.

For example, I can say, "Hi honey," a hundred different ways. I can be angry, sad, sexy, or scared. I can work with objectives and actions, just as I would in a theatrical role. I can need you to comfort me, love me, or leave me. I can be freezing, boiling, or comfortable when I say that. I can be walking, jumping, or dancing when I say it.

When you approach animation ask yourself: Who am I? What do I need? What do I want from everyone in the scene? Use a Meisner approach—really work off your imagined scene partner. Sanford Meisner was an extremely well regarded acting teacher who said for every pinch, there's an ouch, meaning that every truthful moment arises out of an action and a reaction. Connect to your partner; let your partner's imagined reactions pull out your lines. Listen like you would in improv. Let your wants and needs from the other character be the focus, not what you say. In other words, let what you want and need from the other character be so important that you have to say your words in response to their dialogue.

Always study the other character's lines. If you were doing a play you would have to know your cue lines. Make sure you understand every other character's motivation too. So what if you're a crab under the sea—you are still faced with emotional needs. Play them full out.

If you only focus on things like pitch, placement, accent, and age, that's all you'll give an audience. It's like when actors do dialects in plays and can't get to the core of the emotions and needs of the character. Their performance is wooden and flat.

Make Truthful Choices

Practice your scenes in your normal voice. Really invest true emotions. Do substitutions of things in your own life that would create a truthful response. Create *as ifs*, imagining you're doing a scene with someone from your real life. For example, *it's as if my son stole something from a store.* Even if you've got a quick read at your agent's office, try to make it as real for you as you can. Make it a marriage between improvisation and theatre acting techniques that you have practiced. Make quick spontaneous character choices, but also invest real truth to the scene.

Paul Sills commented that actors often want to work from the inside out. He pointed out it can be useful to find inspiration from outside ourselves too.

There are many ways we can use the external world as a source of inspiration. We respond to our environment constantly in everyday life. The *where* in improv can do a lot to define how we behave in a scene. Really play with that element. In a rehearsal, move as your character would. How do they walk—straight or slumped?

Movement is a huge part of character work. As stated before, you can't move too far off mic when you perform voice-overs. However, because you're working at your own pace now, you can rehearse with movements prior to your performance while you're learning to invent characters. Literally going through the motions of their movement and blocking can help you create a more dynamic role. At the mic, you can create the flavor of your background work with minimized stances and facial movements.

Work with external objects. Feel your character's clothing. See objects in your space. Respond to your imagined world. See the facial features of your imagined scene partner. You do this every day but you don't realize it. Think of how you visualize your friend's face when you are talking to her on the phone. Also, recall how you hear past conversations you've had with a friend. Use these examples to help imagine that your scene partners are real, too. It's also what a theatre actor does when they visualize significant objects as anchors on the "fourth wall," the wall that's between the actor and audience. It helps make the room in the scene real and the audience less intrusive. For example, for one role, I put a window in a room to look outside to ignore my annoying family.

You can't just imagine the window, however. You have to fill in the details. Are there curtains? What is right outside the window? Is there activity? It is the actor's job to bring an imaginary world to life and the only way to do this is to fill in the details as you practice. This homework pays off on voice-over jobs because you won't have time to sit and analyze everything.

As my first acting teacher pointed out, if you put a picket fence in the scene in your rehearsal process it will be there when you act. The truth is we don't fully focus on all the layers of our work, but it's still there as a background to the scene. So I might have smelled the grass and heard children in the park when I narrated a scene from my children's book in Central Park. However, I didn't have to sit and imagine every detail. It just came to me. All of my acting homework preparing a myriad of scenes helped me visualize and use my senses very quickly. Simply close your eyes when you prepare in your workouts and see and sense everything in the scene and let your imagination run wild.

Create a notebook with your character and scene breakdowns. Rehearse as many variations at home as possible. What just happened? What was the moment before? What character traits are like you and different from you? Play against type. Really search for real people who help you make your character accessible. Even if you can't do all these things in an audition, the homework exercises will pay off because it will help stimulate your imagination.

Improvise the scene full out using a classic improv game. Create two strips of paper with the first line and the last line of a scene. Then improvise a scene with everything in between. Celebrities excel in animated motion pictures because they can act and create characters that we believe are real. Believe in your characters and others will, too.

Do a back-story for your character. What happened in their lives to bring them to this moment? Do a timeline of your character's life based on the information in the script. How did all the other characters affect their life? Focus on family relationships. Define their work settings and love life. Analyze the script to find all the clues that are there for you to fill in the character in your home workouts.

You'll see why all your acting calisthenics here are so important when you read about the fast-paced animation job scenarios in chapter 6. Remember that anyone can do funny voices but characters like Fred and Wilma entertain us, and we care about them. These characters have a sitcom feel because they are based on Ralph and Alice of *The Honeymooners.* The voice acting style is less cartoonish and closer to a live action feel. Whatever the style, establish a real sincerity at the core of all your animated characters and you're sure to fascinate audiences.

Personal Training Workout

▶ Evaluate all of the following vocal exercises immediately after recording them and then a few days later when you have some distance. Are the characters believable? Do you reach a range of emotions? Note when you just hear a "voice" and not a full-bodied character. Analyze how you can improve your work.

▶ Use the animation scripts in the appendix to practice creating characters and to flex your muscles in the following exercises.

▶ Practice characters from newspaper comic strips or comic books.

- Make sure your characters sound very different.

- Talk back and forth between very distinct characters.

- Improv a monologue for your character.

- Imitate the cartoon characters on TV. (If you imitate just do it for five minutes at a time and take long breaks and drink plenty of water. Since you aren't creating from your own instrument, you can get vocal strain if you aren't connected to your breathing!) Record some shows and play them back with the sound turned down; improv your own character choices, then listen to the character voices in the cartoons.

- Transcribe part of an animation scene. Work on an animated scene in your normal voice. Create truthful choices. Then layer a character voice onto your work.

- Change accents and vocal placements for your character to get out of a *one-note rut*.

- Change the environment or the *where* in the scene to find different colors.

- Work on the overall objectives of your character. List what they want in the whole story and in each scene. Also, list what they want from the other characters in the scene.

- *Break the scene down into beats—or each thought.* For example, (1) I want you to marry me, (2) I want you to make me rich, or (3) I want you to help me escape.

- List a different emotion for each line that you say. For example, happy, greedy, or sad. Imagine you're a kid again playing make-believe in your room. Do an improv of the scene with that state of mind.

- Write out a sketch of your family tree. Imitate and record different family members. *Play around using these core characters as you approach new animation roles.*

- Plot your progress on your characters. What works and what doesn't work? What can you refine and what is ready to use in auditions and bookings?

▶ Draw (if you can) a series of characters. Cut them out and attach them to pens, blunted pencils, or Popsicle sticks. Create voices for your characters. Let them join in conversations in cartoons when you turn the sound down. Practice a variety of copy using your characters' voices.

▶ *Create puppets to talk back and forth to each other.* Pick out two comic strip characters and then talk back and forth between each character.

▶ *Create interior monologues for animals you see on the street.* When you return home write down names for them and add them to your character notebook. Use stuffed animals to improv a story. You can do it like an improv set up. Take *the who, what,* and *where* from magazine strips you cut out. Then just create stories for your characters.

▶ Take objects like cars or furniture and give them voices (this applies to a lot of commercial character work). Perform a scene with the voices you have created and record it.

▶ Now integrate what you've learned to play with a range of audio book characters. Notice how the pace of speech is different in audio books and animation. Also remember books are aural and animation is both visual and aural. Watch TV characters and listen to audio books. The animated characters often speak at a faster pace than many characters in a book. They also may tend to be broader. Get an internal sense of the rhythm with the two different types of characters in each genre.

▶ *The point is, find inspiration to create your very own characters, not just voices.*

·············

Key Web Sites: *www.dawsbutler.com, www.comics.com,* and *www.bobbergen.com.*

See Cartoon Network and Nickelodeon sites.

My Favorite Voice-Over Artists: Bob Bergen, Billy West, Nancy Cartwright, Susan Blu, Melanie Chartoff, Harry Shearer, and Michael J. Fox.

·············

5

The Record Book—Your Demo and Marketing Plan

*S*o, how do you get agents and jobs in the business? Well, first you need the skills to perform a range of copy. Then you need a great demo reel. The demo reel is your calling card to get work, as is the headshot for an actor. You'll spend the most money the first time you do a demo because you have no previous recordings. Once you've booked jobs, you'll be able to cut in new spots and this will cost much less than a full new reel.

The first step you need to take is to go to Voicebank and really observe your competition. Define what you can bring to your demo that can be competitive and reflect all your talent. Then you need to listen to reels created by demo producers. You can usually find demos on their Web site.

A demo producer can help you put it all together. A good demo producer will help you find the right copy, and record and produce the reel. Where do you find a good demo producer? In Los Angeles, the *Voice-Over Resource Guide* lists demo producers. Asking for recommendations in your market is a good way to find the best producer. You can call sound recording studios, talent agencies, and local SAG and AFTRA offices for tips.

When I moved to L.A., I started networking and found at least three sources recommending William "Bill" Holmes, owner of Compost Productions. This is something you want to feel secure about, so take the time to ask. Please remember that demos vary from region to region.

My interview with Holmes provides a good place for you to start to understand the process. You can also refer to chapter 7 for more general information about how producers and agents evaluate demos.

Holmes admits that opinions vary about how to produce a demo but his track record speaks for itself. He says: "We have about an 80- to 90-percent success rate with our demos either getting people work off the demos (enough work to pay for the demo), or getting people agents and they've gone on to do work as well. So if somebody books a job off of our demo, I consider that a victory for us."

The Dos and Don'ts of Demos

First, you do need to get solid direction from a demo producer.

Bill Holmes: "What actors don't realize is that what you're really paying a demo producer to do is to get a good performance out of you, you're paying for their directorial skills as well as their producing skills. So if you go to an engineer who just engineers all day, well, yeah, it's going to sound great, but they're not necessarily a good director, they're not necessarily going to give you good advice about your acting. . . ."

Holmes says the current rates for demos in Los Angeles range from one thousand to two thousand dollars. Therefore he stresses you should feel comfortable and confident with the producer. He says: ". . . don't let people bully you into the demo that they give you." If you ever feel something isn't right, say so. Remember you're a paying customer! Also, don't let someone convince you to do a reel before you are ready.

Bill Holmes: "How do you know when you're ready to make a demo? Well, when you can go into a booth or in a classroom situation, go up to the microphone, you do two takes and then sit down. If you're still up there for twenty minutes and the teacher still has to keep coaxing things out of you, you're probably not ready to make a demo. . . ."

He adds that if you let a director push you into a performance, you may not be able to duplicate the work in an agent's office. You also won't be able to book work because your skills won't match the performance on your demo. What's even worse, if you, by chance, book a job, you'll hurt your reputation if you can't deliver a good performance in a session.

Production Value

Holmes also stresses the importance of not cutting corners. He says an agent will think you're not serious about your career if you pay three hundred dollars for a demo. A good demo producer will spend a lot of time working on your reel.

Bill Holmes: "We're working anywhere from fifteen to twenty-five hours on a demo depending on who we're working with and what level they're at . . . so when you break it down, it's not as much money as it sounds like. You are starting a business, and eighteen hundred dollars is not a lot of money to spend on a new business."

The length of your demo will vary from region to region. You need to listen to demos in your market to be competitive. The demos in Los Angeles tend to be quite short.

Bill Holmes: "An average demo reel these days is between a minute and two minutes, and I would say definitely closer to a minute. You're living in a world of producers who grew up with MTV so their attention span is not too long (same with agents and casting directors and what not). You want the demo reel to be, you know, not boring, basically, you want it to be entertaining."

Once you get an agent, they may ask for a house minute. This is the demo an agent adds to their agency reel to showcase your work.

You will then cut your demo down to sixty seconds. Compost Productions includes this fee in their price. Make sure you know up front if you will be charged to create changes for an agent.

Even if you've never recorded a spot before, your demo needs to replicate the sound of real spots. Rest assured that professional artists also record demo copy to make sure that they showcase their best skills on a reel.

Bill Holmes says: "You kind of want your demo to have a feel that you came to me with a box of commercials that you did in the real world and this is how I had to cut it together."

In order to create a range of realistic spots, you'll need to have some music and effects on spots. Bill Holmes says whether you use these elements or not is all a matter of taste. There are some radio spots that just have a voice track and others have full music and effects. It's important when producing a demo to make sure the demo producer doesn't use the same music for every client. You also want to make sure that your spots don't all sound like they were produced from one studio. This is always a dead giveaway that the spots are not real.

Defining Style and Finding Copy

Most voice-over artists produce a commercial demo reel first. Agents want clients who can do commercial copy. A good commercial reel reflects who you are and generally doesn't include broad characters.

Bill Holmes: "The range of voice is not really that important. . . . don't try to put a range of different types of voices on there—dialects and you know, accents and stuff. Just put a lot of range of just who you are, being quiet and being loud and being silly and being real and being sad, and things like that."

How can you find copy for a demo? Some producers will select copy for you in which case you aren't actively involved in the process.

Bill Holmes: "What I advise people to do is tear ads out of magazines because that is the most current form of advertising out there, and actors have to realize they're going into the advertising business . . . and what magazines? Well, magazines that *you* read . . . because those are the demographics . . . chances are you'll give a better performance, a more honest performance."

Holmes says the amount of time you spend preparing and recording a demo varies. If you have a lot of experience it may take a day to prep your copy. It can also take a year. Some producers will have you rehearse a bit prior to recording your reel and you may record a few hours in a booth. On the other hand, Holmes likes to keep the performance spontaneous and supplies copy at the recording session. In this instance you may record for four hours. Make sure to drink lots of water the day before you record and get plenty of rest the night before your session.

Once the demo is recorded and edited, you need people to evaluate it. Holmes suggests that everyone will not like something but that if everybody likes 65 to 75 percent of your demo, that's good. You need to change something if you hear at least three people comment negatively on the same thing about your reel.

Distributing Your Demo

You may want to get someone to design a CD cover or you may simply do it yourself very professionally (never submit something that does not look like you are a working voice-over artist). You can do a nice logo for your name and make it clean and simple, however, never put your picture on a CD cover. This colors the judgment for your voice. Let your voice say it all. I've also heard that very snazzy covers can be misleading if the voice doesn't match the expectations. Whatever you do with packaging, make sure it matches the demo reel you have created. Go to *www.compostproductions.com* and *www.everythingvo.com* to see some sample designs and get a sense of pricing.

You can also market your demo via an MP3 file on the Internet. I've always asked my demo producer to send me an MP3 file of my reels. You can also convert your CD audio file to an MP3 using iTunes.

Whenever you send out a demo you need to follow up with a call, e-mail, or postcard to make sure it's received. If you don't get a response you can try again. You definitely want to make sure people will listen to your demo but you can only bug people so often and you don't want to be a nuisance. There is no guarantee they will listen but if you have a personal contact, they may want to be polite and are more likely to listen. All you can do with cold submissions is follow up and call back if they say to do so. On the other hand, if you know the person, try to play it for them while you are with them. This is the best way to make sure they hear it.

Years ago at HBO I did that. A colleague said she was helping out with the auditions for the HBO Family Next-Ons. I told her that I had a demo and that it would only take a few moments to listen to it. She followed me to the music room and listened. I got to audition and it helped me want to study my craft more.

Now it's up to you to market the demo at every opportunity!

Showing Off Your Trophies—Marketing

There are many methods to get your voice heard in the marketplace. One of the most effective ways is with a Web site. Cheryllynn Carter, Radio Producer/Voice-Over Casting Director at TBWA Chiat/Day in Los Angeles, sees Web sites as a terrific marketing tool.

Cheryllynn Carter: "Web sites are also a chance to make voices into people rather than tools. On a Web site I can find out about a person. Again it is an opportunity for that person to stay in my head or make their way into a digital folder."

The best way to create an effective Web site is to view your competition. You'll notice some voice actors on Voicebank will have a link directly to their Web site. This sets them apart from other actors. You can see two terrific sites at *www.bobbergen.com* and *www.harlanhogan.com.*

Once again, ask around for a good Web designer. Study what you like and don't like in Web design. I used *www.register.com* because it was a free service with my file transfer protocol site and had twenty-four hour tech support.

I then enlisted the help of a graphic designer I knew from HBO. We already had a great shorthand of communication and she was familiar with marketing. When designing, make sure you can read all your text clearly. I've noticed some sites use colors that are too dark to read.

Chances are a Web site will pay for it self. You will get hits from the Internet and you can send your link out to prospective buyers. Cheryllynn Carter loves the way Web sites help her keep track of talent.

Cheryllynn Carter: "As a producer I am motivated by time, ease, and efficiency. . . . A Web site can be stored digitally so it can go anywhere with me when I need it. . . . Also, I like to be able to look at things when I am ready."

John Matthew is a voice actor and demo producer. You can listen to his interview on the CD that accompanies this book. He's got some great advice about marketing.

John Matthew: "I've found that the most valuable marketing resources are business cards and a Web site. Most work I've had outside the agencies has been from recommendations or clients finding me online. You can send demos to prospects directly, but I've found this to be a very low return activity. Have a good agent, a good demo, a Web site, be good at what you do and market yourself—this is basically how you get most work."

There is no doubt that your best shot at getting work comes from direct contacts you know. If you send out something cold then you have to send probably at least twenty demos to get an audition or job.

Resources and Referrals

Once you have your demo in order, you need to market it. Chances are you want to get an agent. Refer to chapter 8 for more specific tips on acquiring an agent. You may not get an agent right away so you should try to send your demo to as many people as possible who can either get you auditions or bookings. It's always best to have a referral when you send to any possible client, but there are fun ways to make your marketing effective.

Potential client contacts may include: casting directors, production companies, Internet companies, museums, phone prompting companies, in-house corporate production divisions, toy manufacturers, TV and radio stations, and advertising agencies. New technologies emerge all the time; always read the business section of your newspaper to keep abreast of new opportunities. Use a search engine on the Web to find companies in your area. Ask your local Chamber of Commerce if they have a list of local companies.

The Internet is a wonderful tool to use to find new companies if you want to do cold submissions. You can search the Internet for ad agencies in your town, for example. One trick is to look at a casting director's Web site and review their client list. You can then use this list and research the companies.

Use all levels of marketing—e-mail, postcards, letters, phone calls, and CDs. Have fun and market your name and number on pencils, hats, or any item you can think of to put your product in the marketplace. Every person has a favorite and convenient way they take in information. Just as people have different learning styles, people have different moments in the day to take in information. For instance, some people may be more receptive to e-mails when they first arrive at their office on a Monday morning.

It's great to have an e-mail address of potential clients so you can send an MP3, but chances are you may need an inside contact to get the client's address. If you don't have their e-mail address, then send a demo and follow up with a phone call, or postcard, or both. However, be careful not to annoy the person. It's even better if you know someone connected to the client, who can deliver the reel in person.

Be Persistent

Postcards can be sent periodically to reinforce that you're acting and ready to perform. Networking is something you should constantly do.

Many people don't follow through in their marketing because they lack strong organizational skills. You really need to keep track of every postcard, phone call, demo, and MP3 file you send. Index cards or Excel charts can help you sort the list. Send something, then follow up with an e-mail or phone call in about a week. If the company asks you to call back in the future, put it on your calendar and add the information to your catalog system.

I can give examples of using a personal contact and sending something cold. I had heard my friend had gotten a job at Lifetime. Although

I was dead tired from work, I sent a reel right before the Christmas holidays. I thought nothing would come of it because it was the holiday season. In January, I got a call from a producer at Lifetime asking me if I could come in and read for the Billboards. That turned out to be a weekly gig for two and a half years.

When I moved to Los Angeles, I had to navigate my marketing in a huge new territory. I sent my demos to casting directors. I got a call probably six months to a year later to come in for an audition. I didn't have a strong voice-over agent so the audition was a great way to get out and meet people. One of the people I met was John Matthew. He is a voice actor and produces demos through his company, 1042 Voiceworks. We struck up a conversation because I had previously called him to find out about his demo services. John was extremely friendly and I asked him to speak at my UCLA Extension class. Sometime later my husband needed a voice-over talent on short notice for a PBS show. I said, "Use John Matthew." So you can see how referrals work.

I also got another animation audition in Los Angeles from sending my demo. I honestly didn't remember sending my reel but it was a nice surprise to go on the audition. Sending cold to casting directors is a good bet. However, you never know what your client might be like if you send something cold. That's why it pays to check out company Web sites so you have some background information on the client.

Creativity Pays

You can send as many postcards as you want but without an effective marketing strategy it will fall flat. You may reinforce your name with the client, but it will be nothing special. You must let your creativity run wild with your campaigns. I can't think of a better example than the one voice actor Bob Bergen used.

Bob sent around fortune cookies to potential clients that said: "You will soon receive Bob Bergen's demo, who will be perfect for your next ad campaign." Can you imagine sitting at your humdrum job and receiving that fortune cookie? Hey, it lightens your day! It also got Bob Bergen work. People even referred to him as the *fortune cookie guy*. It was a great *branding* campaign.

I know of a woman who bakes brownies and brings them to ad agency people. It's all about entertainment. You've got to come up with

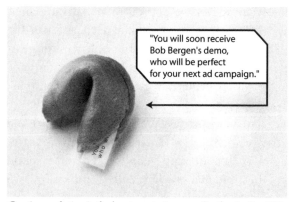

Creative marketing is the key to capturing your client's attention. This fortune cookie idea worked for Bob Bergen. What can you come up with that is fun and different to market your voice-over career? Design by Lisa Lloyd

some *hook* to grab them, make them smile, and even remember you. Otherwise your demo falls into the circular file.

Bill Holmes, who is also a voice actor, used a clever lottery ticket gift idea for agents. The agents remembered it because it was fun and some of them actually won! The point is you've got to *think out of the box*. Go to Jeffery Gitomer's site at *www.gitomer.com*. He gives so many useful offbeat ways to network and market. You can get a lot of good ideas about how to create a hook or brand for yourself.

When I studied with Michelle Danner from the Larry Moss Studio, she said actors have to make their own breaks. Create a local networking event once a month for voice-over talent. Send out a monthly newsletter. Just come up with some creative way to stand out from the crowd. Observe clever print ads, posters, and commercials. Notice how a telemarketer catches you off guard.

Draw on All Your Talents

Finally, what do you do well that can enhance your image and get your name in the marketplace? Do you write well? Can you do graphics? Are you an excellent people person? List everything you do well in this area. Use these skills.

I'm a writer and I've used this skill to write countless letters of introduction, re-connection, and self-promotion to get help. Although I've supervised graphic production, it's not my strong point. Therefore, I seek out people who do it well. This perhaps is the most important thing to know to promote your career. Step back, look at CDs, listen to reels, and watch the pros at work. *List all the things you need to work on and acquire to get yourself known in the business.* In the end, just be yourself. Whether it's hard sell, or a soft sell, know who you are.

Some people can pull off an aggressive approach in hawking their wares, while others have a subtle flair that works like a charm. On the other hand, evaluate the needs of every situation and be able to shift gears if necessary. Build up your hard sell so you'll have it in a more competitive situation. Finesse your moves so you can gently remind someone you're there if the situation calls for it.

Veteran coach and successful voice actress Wendy Dillon always said to remember that you're an actor so you should *use your acting skills to play the situation*. If you're on the phone or meeting people, listen and respond and make it a dialogue, not a monologue. Just like with good acting, you must play the scene. Finally, always be professional and pleasant.

6

Playing Your Game

*N*ow that you have a sense of a range of genres, it's important to explore the practical side of recording each style. You'll shade your acting choices by the nuances of each genre. However, the audition process has some similar traits. Whether you go to an agent's office to audition or you record from home, you'll have to adjust your work to the specs, or creative direction, and character description of the script. For example, a commercial may ask for a sultry low voice with authority. On the other hand, an animation script may call for a nervous loyal insecure lamb.

In both cases, you must at least fulfill the specs on the first take. The creative team wants to hear that. Give your own interpretation or follow the director's advice for take two. Make sure to make new choices in your second take to show your acting range.

As stated before, you have to slate your name and the product or character. For example, I'd say "Janet Wilcox HBO take one," or "Janet Wilcox Daisy take one." This identifies your work so clients can call you and book you.

Game Time—Auditions

When you are just starting out, you're more likely to go to a casting director or agent for direction. If you have very little experience you'll need the added input so don't audition from home before you have some performance chops. You may receive scripts via e-mail a day prior to an audition at home or at a studio. On the other hand, you may have to wait to receive scripts until you go to your agent's office. Voice actor Bob Bergen describes how many scripts a working actor might have to prepare if he shows up at the agent's office one-half hour prior to his audition.

Bob Bergen: "Let's say once you get there you are handed seven pieces of copy: one TV spot, three radio spots, two characters for a new cartoon, and a television promo. You have thirty minutes to create the characters, dissect the commercials, figure out your delivery for the promo, etc. If your agent is running on time you'll have less than five minutes per script to prepare. If this sounds overwhelming you aren't ready to pursue voice-over. Voice-over isn't cold reading, it's frozen. Because of this, voice-over actors are some of the best actors in show biz."

If you're a working voice actor, you may audition as much as five times a day or as little as a few times a week. You may get a call the day before or an hour before a gig. A casting director, agent, or booth director may direct you or you might audition from home without direction.

At your first audition, relax and breathe. Be polite but don't waste anyone's time. Show up at least thirty minutes early and find a secluded place to rehearse, and sign in once you are ready, before your assigned time. Focus and perform in the booth, then thank your director and be on your way. Whether you get a callback or other audition varies for different genres; often you do not.

When you receive a booking varies for each project. That's why it's important to tell your agent if you aren't available and have to "book out" for any period of times. I've booked jobs in the same week as an audition and several weeks later. In the voice-over business, you have to be ready for anything.

Technical High Hurdles

Once you are actually out there getting auditions (and booking jobs), you will have to deal with a number of different technical issues, as well as different procedures and expectations, depending upon what kind of a job you are up for, and what kind of a business is producing the job (Ad agency? Network? Animation studio?). Remember that you will perform in a booth behind glass. Don't let the isolation distract you on your first job. When the engineer asks for a sound check, read with the same volume you will perform the script. Also, be courteous to the engineer because he can make you sound better or worse.

Voice to Picture

One of the techniques that you will have to master is a voice to picture recording. This technique may be used in a number of genres. For example, you may have to read a promo script to a temporary audio guide track and match it to the visuals of spot. Or, you may have to do ADR (automated dialogue replacement) for a character in an animation job. That is when you have to read your part and match it to the character's mouth movements on screen. Veteran actor Bob Bergen describes how you do this in the booth.

Bob Bergen: "When doing ADR, you record one line of dialogue at a time. You watch the scene while wearing headphones. You will hear three consecutive beeps in your headphones. You begin recording on the fourth imaginary beep. This is for timing purposes. It gets you into the scene at the proper moment. So it's 'beep, beep, beep,' act!! And it's OK to need a couple of takes to get it right. No one is expected to be perfect in one take."

This is an advanced technique and I'll give you some fun exercises to play around with on page 99. Basically, you have to look at a script very quickly when you receive it and then get the sense of rhythm of the visuals and the guide track and mimic the flow, all with little prep time. For example, the one-hour E! Show I narrated, *Hollywood & Divine*, was a voice to picture job. I received the script right before I walked into the booth. Therefore, there was little time to rehearse and the client also gave last minute changes. The show had a rough temporary (scratch) track of the narration and sound bites of interviews in the show. I would use the scratch track and pictures to guide my pacing and start reading after a sound bite concluded.

This is precisely why you do a strong home workout. If you have some advance notice for this kind of work, you can record other shows from your client and transcribe them. Then do your home version of a voice to picture read so you'll get comfortable with the process. You'll have to practice splitting your focus between the picture and your script. Glance at the picture for rhythm, and then learn to read smoothly without losing your place.

Promos: Precision Delivery

There's no time to waste in a promo session. A voice actor must have primed articulation skills and an excellent sense of timing. Tiesha Brunson, Director, ABC Daytime, On-Air Promotions, describes how the network acquires voice talent.

Tiesha Brunson: "We call the agencies and tell them what kind of voice we're looking for. Then we give them a script(s) to read. Usually, people are referred, but mostly we go through an agency."

You must be ready to perform quickly in promo sessions. You'll usually be in a session with a promo producer and a sound engineer. You may have one spot to read or a stack of scripts on your copy stand. At HBO, we often did one script in a half-hour session, but at A&E we might do at least three scripts in that time.

Tiesha Brunson: "In one session, we will read as little as one fifteen-second promo or as much as three promos ranging from five to thirty seconds. . . . Usually, we do about two to five takes for a thirty-second promo—depending on the complexity of it."

You have to be flexible too. Promo scripts match the tone of each show or campaign and can have a range of styles and pacing.

Tiesha Brunson: "The VO talent definitely needs to have range. He/she needs to be able to sound dramatic for the dramatic promos, comedic for the funny promos and trailer-like for the primetime-y feel promos. They also need to have a sense of timing. If we need something read in a certain amount of time, they need to be able to hit that mark."

The talent can receive a few hours notice for a session booking or may be called the afternoon before a 9 A.M. recording. Voice actors also may be called in on short notice due to revisions. You need to understand that network executives have to approve spots before they can be recorded. Rates vary from a few hundred dollars for a session fee to several hundred thousand dollars a year if you have a contract.

Every network works differently. At HBO we always did the voice track first and then we cut the picture. ABC Daytime Promotion does a voice to picture recording. It's important to have a strong aural memory to call on when you perform.

Tiesha Brunson: "Usually when the VO talent comes into the room, I let them know the style of read that I'm looking for and any words that I want him/her to emphasize. Then I let them read it. If needed, I will give direction. The VO talent can usually see the promo while they're reading it. They usually get three beeps before they begin their read."

Be Ready to Perform

The most important thing to remember is that spots may go on the air the same day or following day after you record. This is possible because everything but the final voice track has been reviewed and approved by network executives. The voice track is one of the last things added to the spot prior to airing it. Promo producers can't take a chance on amateurs. You must hit your marks and be a team player.

Tiesha Brunson: "Voice actors shouldn't be late for their session. They shouldn't tell the producer how they want to read something. They shouldn't try to re-write the script. They should know how to follow direction."

Promo work can be steady and consistent. It's a lot like theatre work because top-notch voice actors perform several days a week. It's also wonderful having a steady paycheck! I know I loved doing the weekly Lifetime Billboard gig! Your chops are primed and you're always ready to perform.

Commercials: Patience and Flexibility

It's rare that you'll book a commercial without auditioning and you may have a callback. Cheryllynn Carter of Chiat Day in Los Angeles says she'll only consider a voice actor without an agent if they have a specialized talent she has to fill. She describes a typical week.

Cheryllynn Carter: "For an average radio script I get my estimate signed and a script and casting specs on Monday. I send that out on Monday to get voices by Wednesday. My creative makes his choice and then the client approves them by end of day Thursday and I record on Friday or Monday. I hardly have time to audition, so callbacks are just a dream."

Every minute is precious in the fast-paced advertising world. Therefore, your audition needs to stand out and also match the specs.

Cheryllynn Carter: "I hear anywhere between 150 to 350 auditions for one spot. I cut that down to about thirty and that is all my creative hears."

Imagine listening to all those auditions! The patience can wear thin with actors who don't deliver.

Cheryllynn Carter: I have a saying. "You are only as good as your last audition. That goes for actors and agents. If I send a script to an agent and he sends me thirty voices and none of them work at all I will not send that agent another script. I do not have time to spend on thirty voices that do not work."

You Booked It!

Cheryllynn says a recording session may be a half hour or an hour. A voice actor has to be prepared to perform in front of a group of people behind the glass. A performer must deliver as many as one hundred takes if necessary.

Cheryllynn Carter: "There have been days when I have had four account people, the client, the client's intern, my creative, his intern, myself, and my assistant at the session."

It's important to be patient with so many takes. Often the agency creative team is trying to cover all the possibilities the client may want. Just remember the client pays for everything and you should be happy to flex your acting muscles! Carter gives an example of a TV rate. "A voice-over talent doing a national spot for TV could make anywhere from three thousand dollars to five thousand, depending on the spot. Gold mine spots are: car commercials, feminine hygiene commercials, insurance commercials, and fast food commercials." Keep in mind that if a spot airs in a lot of markets, a VO talent could make $20,000.

Pacing for Long Form Reads

Documentaries, shows, and industrials require great stamina and sharp diction. You can learn more about this work from John Matthew's interview on the CD. John narrated over forty-five shows for the *Food Network*. Although every job is different, you can get a sense of this work from John's stories here. He said there may or may not be callbacks from auditions. Most of the work he has done has been cast through agencies, but he has had some direct bookings from clients.

You can refer to the appendix for rates or go to the Voice-Over Resource Guide Web site. An example of a non-union pay range may be around $350 to two thousand dollars, without residuals, depending on the length of the program. On the other hand, you always have to calculate residuals for union jobs. For example, you might make an $894 session fee for a one-hour network TV program and additional $670.50 with residuals if it plays another cycle.

Longer Recording Sessions

The shows John Matthew narrated were not voice to picture. Here he describes a typical session.

John Matthew: "We generally took about two hours to record a one-hour show. That included a few minutes to chat at the top of the session, plus a five-minute break. . . . We usually did two takes per graph, with the occasional third take here or there. Four was rare. . . . I chose to sit to record the FN shows, as my neck and shoulders would tighten up pretty quickly and two hours was way too long to stand."

Production deadlines dictate when you will receive a script.

John Matthew: "I would get at least a day or two with the script; later on it got tighter and often I would receive the script by e-mail the day of the session."

There is no magic bullet to make a session run smoothly, but John Matthew gives some great tips.

John Matthew: "There really aren't any "tricks" to speak of. It's just doing good work: reading through the script (out loud) is a must, come up with your own marking system for pauses, emphasis, inflection, etc.— this is definitely helpful. Watch the rough cut (if available) and internalize the subject matter so you know what you're talking about. Watch the finished products and listen for what worked and what didn't in your performance. Make sure your reading chops are up so your diction is clear and unforced, and you can last for two hours in the studio if you need to. In other words—practice!"

John gives great advice. Please be sure, however, not to over stress the voice the day before a recording session. You should work on building up your skills before you book jobs.

Flexing Your Acting Muscles for Books

Do you love literature? Does it transport you into another place and time? Agile actor Richard Allen reads audio books for Penguin-Putnam, Random House, and Brilliance Audio. He was on Broadway in *Ragtime*. Like many book narrators, he comes from a strong acting background. Allen says, "You have to be able to read one hundred pages a day." He admits there are days when the lung capacity and vocal strength aren't up to par, but you should strive to get close to one hundred pages. Sessions may run from four to eight hours a day.

Most people sit to read the manuscript but every reader is different. Allen says some people like to read for four hours while others like to "crank." Some readers may make two or three mistakes a page while others are legends in the field.

Richard Allen: "There are people we know and love, they are machines and they can just read seven, eight, or twelve pages and not make a mistake."

Compare that to your reading skills if you are interested in narrating books. Allen says that if a reader chooses to do an eight-hour day then they will take an hour for lunch and get ten-minute breaks every time the engineer changes a CD. You can figure that a page runs approximately two minutes and a CD runs about sixty-eight to seventy-five minutes.

Research and Rehearsals

Richard says you may have one or two weeks to prepare a book for your recording session. This gives you time to read the work aloud and make character choices. He also says you can mark the manuscript.

Richard Allen: "You have to make your own marks, because the way that a writer writes and the way a narrator narrates that writing are often very different."

So that's a fairly relaxed rehearsal process. On the other hand Allen says that if there is a crash, you're going to get about three days. Therefore, you may have to prepare one hundred pages out loud the night before you read.

How do you create and keep all the characters straight? Richard says there are a couple of rules of thought. Some people write out character-izations on the side of the page. He also says you can get a sense of the characters from the author's descriptions. You may have to research the character's background too.

Allen says he always calls the library or chamber of commerce of the character's hometown because most staff people in municipalities are natives to the town in which they work.

This is a great tip to research regional characters. Because a book has so many characters, you have to have a good ear. You must be able to do as many accents as the book requires. As Richard notes, a director will listen while you record and make sure that your characters are consistent and you keep true to the text.

You must also have the technical acting skills to create characters quickly and perform scenes with the appropriate dramatic range. The best way to learn this is by performing plays or play readings.

Marketing and Money

First, you have to understand that voice actors narrate either abridged or unabridged books. The abridged books often are sold in retail stores like Barnes & Noble so stars often narrate them. This work pays more. Richard says a publisher like Penguin-Putnam or Simon & Schuster may pay anywhere from three thousand to five thousand dollars for a first-rate voice actor.

On the other hand, unabridged books may be placed in libraries. Richard points out that the pay is less but the quality of the work does not suffer. He says the reads for these books are so good because: "Sometimes you'll get a journeyman actor who will put in the time" to do good work.

A non-union job may pay around five hundred to one thousand dollars for the gig. You can consult the union rates in the appendix on page 183. Just keep in mind that the union rates are for each completed hour of recording. Allen says an average book, which is anywhere from two hundred thirty and three hundred pages, is approximately four hours long.

You get this work by all means possible. You audition, use an agent, and submit demos. Do your research on audio book publishers on their Web sites. Call the audio publisher and find out whom to contact to send a demo. Do the same with agents and find out which ones represent actors for audio books.

Richard says you don't have to live in New York or Los Angeles to do audio books. The opportunities abound across America for this work. Richard says some publishers like Simon & Schuster have audio book divisions. On the other hand, Blackstone Books in Oregon only does audio books. There's work with the Library of Congress. Of course, you may make more money in New York and Los Angeles than you do in other locations.

The only way to be successful in getting this work is to do a great demo. The demo should include a recording of a few pages of a book that showcases your unique talent and demonstrates your range. You also have to have a good flow to the read.

Pick out books that you do well. Richard says your demo may include two-minute selections of consecutive pages for each genre on your reel. Your reel may include a range of selections such as: standard fiction, non-fiction, a biography, romance, self-help, or comedy. You now have an idea of what it takes to narrate audio books. My advice is to practice and record as often as possible if you want to pursue this work.

The Rhythm and Flow of Teamwork

Multiple character radio spots can be a dream job because you'll probably get to work in the booth with other actors. That interplay can be fun and feel more like traditional acting than other kinds of jobs. Nonetheless, you'll work quickly and probably not have a chance to get to know your scene partner. On the other hand, Arif S. Kinchen, voice-over artist and on-camera actor, says to make sure to take advantage of any spare moment you have to get to chat.

Arif S. Kinchen: "What I like is when they leave you in the booth for more than ten minutes and you're able to sit there and yap with the other actor and get some common ground."

You generally get auditions for this work from casting directors and agents. Actors slate their names in the order their characters appear in the script. For example, if my character has the first line, I'll say, "Janet Wilcox, Betty."

Arif points out that you need to be ready for anything, from line reads to rewrites. You also may share the booth with quite a few actors. He just auditioned for a spot with six actors and there were two mics in the booth. In this instance, you have to learn to step into the mic to deliver your line and then back away when someone else performs a line. Arif says it's necessary to respect your fellow actors. On the other hand, I encourage you to find your space and not be off cue. When you're starting out you may be timid and miss your cue. Resist this urge and get to the mic on time.

Chances are, when you book the job, you'll work with your scene partner in the booth. However, you may also hear cue lines from actors in a distant studio in the "cans" or headphones via ISDN. I know of actors who have had to deliver lines wild, too, after hearing a recorded cue line once. In other words, the actor records the line out of sequence apart from the other actors in the scene. Therefore, it's important to have a strong aural memory when you perform, because they may only play the cue lines once.

As with all union work, the total payment varies how often a spot is on the air, so there is no set rate.

Cheryllynn Carter: "A talent in LA gets approximately four hundred dollars for a session payment. That covers the first thirteen weeks of air-play. Then if the spot needs to run past that one to three weeks, they get another four hundred dollars. Most radio spots do not run much longer then that. So, my guess would be about eight hundred dollars. However, if there are different versions of the spot made, and tags, etc., that multiplies by the number of spots." Tags are the lines added at the end of spots for specific tailoring. For example, a tag may give regional information for a product or offer.

Bonus Points

Sometimes actors can cash in on unexpected opportunities. Arif was given the chance to record lines for two different characters for a bank spot. The characters said things like: "Hey great" and "Really free online banking!"

In another instance, Arif had an audition at a sound studio. The spot had a lot of ambience background lines to create the real feel of the Department of Motor Vehicles. Some of the actors were paid as if they booked the job because their auditions were used in the final spots, adding to the ambient background sound!

I confess, this is my favorite kind of spot, but you really have to bring realistic acting choices to play. You also have to pick up your cues. I find beginners often don't respond fast enough to their cue lines. There is no time to think, you have to respond right a way. Remember radio spots are sometimes thirty seconds long.

Animation—Acting on the Spot

Agents are essential if you want to do animation work and most of the jobs are in Los Angeles. Voice actor Bob Bergen says: "There's no way of knowing what is being cast without an agent." Callbacks are common and can occur anywhere from the next day to months or weeks later.

Bob Bergen: "Your agents will call you into their office to read the copy. They then send the auditions via e-mail sound files to the casting directors. The casting director then will call you back to read in person. . . . The hardest part is remembering what you did. The best advice I can give an actor when getting a callback is to do exactly what they did at the first audition unless directed otherwise."

It's important to understand how quickly you may have to perform once you book a job.

Bob Bergen: "As for bookings, for an animated series they might send you the script the day before. . . . And I've had some who just hand me the script when I arrive at the studio to record."

Once you've done your homework, you'll need to be ready to perform at the recording session. Rehearsals vary from a full run-through prior to recording to no rehearsal at all. You probably won't record one hundred takes like you might in a commercial, but you'll do as many as the director deems necessary.

Bob Bergen: "There isn't much rehearsal at all, either way. Often times the second time the words come out of the actor's mouth is the printed take. For a thirty-minute animated series, they have you for four hours to record the episode. For an animated feature, the contracts are for eight-hour days. And an animated feature can take anywhere from one to five years from recording to in the theaters. An episode for a series is usually about a year from recording to on air."

Pretend Your Partner Is There

You may be recording your part alone in the booth if you're recording the voice before the picture is animated.

Bob Bergen: "I play Bucky the squirrel in *The Emperor's New Groove*, as well as the spinoff series *The Emperor's New School*. Patrick Warburton, Putty of *Seinfeld* fame, plays Kronk. He and I have many scenes together with great chemistry. We've actually never recorded in the same room, and only met for the first time a few months ago. But when edited together we are Abbott and Costello."

On the other hand, you may have to replicate a pre-recorded character's work if you do ADR work as discussed previously. Actors often dub in voices for anime characters.

Bob Bergen: "You need to watch the scene, read the copy, match sync, and act all at the same time."

Finally, Bergen gives some great tips on conversing with yourself if you do multiple characters.

Bob Bergen: "If you are playing more than one character in a series you might have a two-way conversation with yourself. You record the script in order from beginning to end. My record was seven characters in one episode. And I had a seven-way conversation with myself. It's not easy!! I like to give each character a different facial expression, different body language, etc., so as not to blend the voices from line to line."

You may also transfer these techniques to recording characters for video games. Remember this is an interactive medium so you'll have to record all the options for the characters. For example the lines may be: "Go this way, come with me," or "Stop right there!" Think of this as a game as you encourage or chide the player and it may be more fun. However, as Bob Bergen warns, there may be a lot of yelling in video game sessions! Make sure to take good care of your voice and rest afterwards.

Refer to the pay rates in the appendix to get an idea of what you can earn for different animation jobs. Bob Bergen gives an example of a rate an actor might earn on a union animation series that airs without residuals. He says, "The minimum you'd make on a thirteen week run is your session fee of $9,308."

Game Time—Thinking Outside the Booth

How can you emulate the aforementioned actors on the job? Always say positive things to yourself in the booth and play on. It's also important to review and know what works or doesn't work for you. Keep a mental notebook of the times you run into trouble. Maybe you didn't allow enough prep time for the audition. On the other hand, on a good day you may have used strong cues to fill your imagination and it worked. Just try to review and renew. Keep a notebook handy after auditions and bookings and log your observations.

There is only one thing that should come to mind. It's the same improv rule, "Yes, and." Simply give in to it and say, "Yes, and I'll make it faster," or more dramatic or whatever. I just had an interview with the engineer at Ives Creative today. He said he just wants the talent not to yell into the mic or laugh too loud or refuse to follow direction. He hears enough excuses from voice actors and just wants them to do what he asks. *You've got to listen and respond.* Isn't that rule number one of acting?

See it as a challenge. The game is tied . . . you've got to punt . . . it's the playoffs. You are an actor. *Your lifeblood is transforming yourself in new situations.*

Believe it or not, you can lift the spirits of your co-workers. They're under this stress you can't imagine. Help them out, they'll appreciate your attitude and professionalism and maybe even get home to dinner on time.

Finding Work

Are you just starting out? Then you'll need to be a good researcher. Although your main goal is to get an agent, that doesn't always happen right away. (I'll give tips on finding an agent more fully in chapter 8.) Therefore, you need to study the work scene in your region while you try to get an agent. Know your client sources. As stated in the previous chapter, use an Internet search engine to research potential clients in your area. Cultivate relationships with people who can tell you something you don't know. Even if an agent won't sign you, if you can meet one or are lucky enough to have lunch with one, learn all you can.

Most large cities have organizations that record newspapers or books for the blind. SAG has Book PALS. Be creative; you can read to children at libraries and bookstores, or read to the elderly. The point is to do something. Create an opportunity if you have to do so. Play readings also are great. Volunteer at a radio station, ad agency, or talent agency if you can afford to do it. You may want to respond to casting ads. *Back Stage* magazine, CraigsList, *www.wheresspot.com*, and *www.entertainmentcareers.net* list voice-over jobs. You'll most likely need to demo copy for the audition on an MP3.

In regard to paid work, pay scales for work varies from genre to genre and rates change with new contracts. Therefore, it's best for you to refer to the current rates for each type of work at *www.VoiceOverResourceGuide.com.* You can turn to page 183 for sample rates at the time of this publishing. Please understand that these are basic union rates only, but they are a good benchmark for pay. A session fee is what you're paid when you record in the booth. Then you will receive residuals based on where your work is played and how often it plays.

Today there also is another source of mostly non-union work through Internet services. You usually pay a one-time fee for a year to get leads for jobs. You then audition via an MP3 file. You essentially pay a fee to pick and choose auditions. It's almost like an Internet agent. I have heard good word of mouth and know several people who have booked through *www.voice123.com*. Another service to check out is *www.interactivevoices.com*, which has a range of voice-over auditions where you bid for the jobs.

You can submit a demo directly to writers, producers, and directors, too. You can find their names on TV credits if you don't know anyone. Again, it's best to have a recommendation from someone. How do you do this? To start out, just list the people you know who can help you with your career. Take a week and write a list of everyone you know who has connections to people in the entertainment business. Tell them you're doing voice-overs and see if they can't pass the reel on for you.

Send your demos to casting directors; they can call you in without an agent. You can find them listed in the *Ross Reports* and in the *Voice-Over Resource Guide* in Los Angeles. SAG and AFTRA may have lists in your area. Research documentary companies and radio stations on the Web to find out who hires or auditions talent. You can also find lists of companies in trade books like *The Hollywood Creative Directory*. Sound studio engineers may know people and pass your reel to producers. Use a search engine on the Internet and find recording studios in your area.

Never underestimate the power of doing favors for people. You can record *scratch* tracks for producers. These are the first tracks an editor uses to guide him in cutting the picture. It's basically a placeholder. Once the spot is cut, a voice-over artist will record the final version. Editors could be a great source to get experience for those opportunities.

Obviously, personal industry contacts are important. You can use the Web as a tool to learn about industry groups. Volunteer to help with film and TV functions. Get to know people.

Always read for the blind; it pays you back in hundreds of ways no paycheck can.

The High Bar: Advanced Personal Training Workout

It's important to always keep your eyes on the page when you read. However, here are some ways to prepare for voice-to-picture jobs.

▶ Take the lyrics of a song you have heard and practice lip-syncing to a recording in front of a mirror. Work at lifting the lines off the page and looking in the mirror. In other words, you have to glance at the words and memorize enough so that you can say it and look up to make sure your mouth is in sync with the words. You split your focus so you can check that you're in sync and that you don't miss any words on the page.

▶ You can do this to a music video and work on your lip sync skills. *Music is an excellent tool because you'll learn if you tend to run ahead or behind the beat.*

▶ You can then transcribe spots and shows that you have recorded (or send away for transcribed shows) and practice splitting your focus from the page to the screen. Work on becoming more and more proficient at this. Raise the bar again. Try it ice cold once. This exercise is useful because you work on your timing skills. You must hit your mark.

▶ For dubbing, watch a commercial and mirror what the on–camera talent says as closely as possible as you listen to the voice.

▶ Next, practice taking a transcribed script and recorded spot and match your read to the on–camera speaker's lip movements.

▶ Reach higher. Do the last exercise with an animation character. As you become more proficient try it with less and less prep time.

▶ Always evaluate your work and notice if you're in sync or out of sync in these exercises.

7

Coaches' Corner

*O*kay, I've given a basic introduction to voice-over. *Now learn about the industry from the pros in different areas of the business.* It's important to know what agents, casting directors, sound experts, and executives who hire voice-over talent think about the field. Learn from some excerpts I've obtained from a cross-section of veterans in the business.

What Makes a Successful Voice-over Talent?

Wes Stevens (voice-over agent, VOX, Inc., Los Angeles): "An individual of intellect, wit, and creativity. Someone who can roll with the punches, live in the moment, and organically bring copy to life. Above all they have a singular point of view and they understand the nuance of whatever aspect of this industry they are performing in. . . ."

Bob Bergen (voice actor, voice of Porky Pig, teacher): "Acting, acting, acting!!! No matter what kind of VO work you are trying to break into, it's all about the acting. . . . The obvious trait that animation voice actors have is the ability to change their voice to match characters . . . you have to be believable. There is no such thing as a good voice! Everyone has a good voice! If you listen to radio and TV you hear very real, non-announcer-y, guy/gal next door reads. It's oh so much harder to be real than it is to be announcer-y!"

Terry Berland (Terry Berland Casting in Los Angeles, casting director, teacher and author): "A good talent can give slight variations. A good talent has every moment figured out without it sounding so."

Cynthia Songe (voice actress, casting director at Blupka Productions, Los Angeles, demo producer and teacher): "Authenticity. As my mentor, Susan Blu defines our job: 'reading giving the illusion that we are not reading.' To bring as much of ourselves, our personality to the copy. It is a wonderful industry that allows us to celebrate our uniqueness of spirit without the judgment of the physical."

Marilyn McAleer (a creative director at HBO and Cinemax, National Geographic Worldwide, and vice president of advertising and promotion for Lifetime Television, now a consulting agent and director of marketing for the Atlas Talent Agency, New York City): "A good natural read (an actor's performance) is essential. A distinction in the voice, like good clear bell-like tones or more texture to stand out. Also, the tools that clearly identify a unique personal attitude and style."

Selena Smith, National Agent (SAG-Aftra) at John Robert Powers International, answered the same question in regard to regional talent: "Excellent verbal skills, the ability to listen and take direction. The drive and determination. Above all else, [a] strong business sense. Voice-over talent are truly *Voice-over actors*, people who study acting and improv seem to be able to interpret copy better. Just because people tell you that you have a great voice doesn't mean you can sell a product or an idea."

What Makes a Good Voice-over Demo?

Michael Maxwell (producer, composer, owner of Pink Noise Studio, New York City): "What usually grabs my attention are professional-sounding examples of what they sound like and what turns me off is the opposite. For me to sell an actor to a client, I've got to have good sounding examples."

Terry Berland: "A well-packaged CD gets my attention and certainly any recommendation from either another actor or agent whom I respect will get me to listen."

Wes Stevens: "I listen to referrals only. My office listens to everything and passes along candidates that make sense for all of us to hear. That's probably about one demo out of every couple hundred. I vastly prefer MP3s, so a cover makes little difference to me.

"There is nothing more annoying than excessive packaging, gimmicks. Packing peanuts are a tremendous no-no. I wear a lot of black and I don't like lint.

"I have never understood why anyone would submit something that was not of superior production value. We are in a highly dynamic, audio business, if it doesn't sound real, why send it out? The first seconds have to pop, have to suck us in . . . if it is not there in the first seconds, I'm done. I don't make it more than ten seconds into many demos."

Bob Bergen: "It's a cyber world now. Web sites are a great way to market! Agents have 'em, plus there's Voicebank, which has every VO agent represented with all their client's demos. Also, when ready, study with those who cast! It's the best way for them to get to know you and your talents."

Marilyn McAleer: "First the CD cover . . . It must be aesthetically pleasing and professional. Weak visuals offend me. Not enough information and an unprofessional attitude on the CD offend me. All I want is to hear the product and determine if it matches my needs."

Cynthia Songe: "I do get many, many demos. I listen to most of them with no particular pattern . . . it usually depends on my casting schedule. Sometimes I listen as they come in, sometimes in groups at a sitting. Yes, referrals might make a demo rise to the top of the listening pile quicker. I am appreciative of CD artwork but all I truly care about is a big bold legible name . . . fancy artwork means nothing if the demo isn't good . . . as a matter of fact it makes it stand out more."

Here's how people prefer receiving demos:

Michael Maxwell: "CDs definitely."

Cynthia Songe: "Either [CDs or MP3s]. I have primarily been getting CDs."

What Are Your Pet Peeves?

Pros have issues with voice actors. You can learn a lot by reading these comments.

Here is one of the things that annoys Terry Berland about voice-over actors: "Not reading instructions or directions written to them outside of the room as far as what the read should be. Another one is an actor who [doesn't] like a late afternoon time (times close to 5 P.M.). They come early to get out early to avoid the evening traffic. The session gets backed up and we have many more people than we can handle waiting to audition."

Cynthia Songe: "Funny voices not believable characters. Being too 'on.' Not taking the leap to commit . . . letting fear hold them back."

Marilyn McAleer: "Many voice actors are too precious about their art and have an enormous sense of entitlement. They don't understand their buyer's needs and therefore can't focus on giving them what they need and often don't acknowledge that they don't have what the buyers need."

Selena Smith: "Do you mean whiny, crybaby, 'Why aren't I working,' pain-in-my-butt voice-over talent?"

What Are the Biggest Mistakes Actors Make?

Bob Bergen offers advice about not rushing to do things before you are ready.

Bob Bergen: "The biggest mistake I see actors make is making a demo and sending it out before they are ready. This is a very unforgiving business. There are very few VO agents in Los Angeles, and they have a very long memory. . . . Make your demo when you are absolutely ready.

"In L.A., 90 percent of your auditions are in your agent's office. . . . If you have a home studio you can send in your own MP3. . . . I don't recommend beginners read from home. You need the direction! You also need to be visible to your agent! Don't put in a home set up until you are a working actor! And if animation is your thing then you must live in Los Angeles. Almost all of it is recorded here."

What Skills Do VO Actors Need?

Professionals notice that many voice-over artists lack strong skills to help them succeed.

Cynthia Songe: "Technically speaking, the ability to be truly conversational rather than announcer-y . . . and, of course, not to judge ourselves or listen to ourselves. It's like trying to be on stage with a third eye watching yourself, you just can't do that and be authentic. The same thing goes for voice actors . . . we must be in it, doing it, authentically (that word again) and not listening to ourselves."

Terry Berland: "Acting skills. In the beginning the talent has to listen to direction, interpret the direction and then have their instrument obey their own direction."

Marilyn McAleer: "Energy and voice control."

Wes Stevens: "A point of view. Commitment to the moment. The ability to see the audition as the gig . . . getting hired and paid is gravy."

In regard to regional talent Selena Smith adds this comment: "Thinking inside the box. Not listening to their agents."

What's It Like to Be on Your Side of the Desk?

Many actors are unaware of the pressures casting directors and agents face. Maybe these comments will help you understand how you can help them do their jobs and succeed in the business.

Terry Berland: "We are given very little time to prep a session. We usually get ten to fifteen dropouts and another ten people who have to change their times. We try to juggle everything to accommodate the actors and have a nice full session for our clients. Everything gets backed up. Actors get irritated and we're pedaling as fast as we can so we don't have to pay overtime and have our clients pay overtime."

Wes Stevens: "We are genuinely committed to our clients' careers and we want them to succeed, we want them to have 'careers.' That passion is pressure unto itself."

Cynthia Songe: "That we can only cast one person for the role. Soooo much talent that is wonderful, but only one person gets the job. As Susan [Blu] says, remember: 'It's selection, not rejection.' Something I have to remind myself when I'm on the other side of the glass as an actor."

Are Celebrities Monopolizing the Field?

It's easy to say celebrities get all the work. This is what the pros have to say about celebs in the business:

Bob Bergen: "The reason why it seems there are so many more celebs doing VO now is because there is so much more product out there. . . . And even though it might feel like celebs are taking all of our work, trust me folks, there's plenty to go around. Non-celebs need to concentrate on training, making a great demo, getting a great agent, and marketing!"

Marilyn McAleer: "I don't think celebrities will eventually do all voice-over work. Buyers go to celebrities for brand prestige and audience interest in a competitive market. . . . They're very expensive. . . . Non-celebrity voices are a more economical choice. You can get a great read and voice at 5 percent of the money or less. Celebrity voices are a crapshoot—you can't ask for an audition, it's take it or leave it. I think many producers have gotten themselves into a jam by soliciting celebrity voices, settling and being unable to admit how bad the voice is to their clients."

What Are Your Thoughts about the Agent/Client Relationship?

Here are some things an actor should expect from an agent.

Marilyn McAleer: "Talent should expect an agent to give him/her opportunities . . . frequent auditions to compete for projects within the agency from the agency's buyer network . . . talent should expect they get the best rate in an environment where rates are diminishing. They should expect meetings with agents every six months to determine if they're on track and if not, to strategize on a plan to get it back on track."

Cynthia Songe: "With an agent we should have the ability to have a good relationship . . . it is an important business marriage. It is equally important to show our talent and be the best we can be as it is to trust their expertise. The relationship should be on equal ground . . . where both parties do their best, have dialogue and value each other."

Here's how agents help on-camera talent transition to voice-over.

Selena Smith: "We have them study the skills and ways of the top-booking VO talent. Then just change the organic element of the acting experience."

On the other hand, here's what agents want from talent.

Marilyn McAleer: "Agents expect their clients to recognize that they are in a competitive world and they are responsible for improving and enhancing their own skills. . . . Agents can certainly help a client in determining a marketing plan but if a client isn't bringing revenue into the agency, they should be prepared to implement their own plan."

What about the Actor's Relationship to the Casting Director?

Casting directors give you very special opportunities. Here are some examples of the unique things they do in the business:

Cynthia Songe: "The casting director works very close with the advertising team. It is their job to fulfill the advertising teams' intention."

Terry Berland: "Actors like to audition directly with casting directors because the casting session will have approximately thirty to fifty people per role (depending on the circumstance). When the breakdown is given out to agents the actor is usually up against hundreds of other people."

Casting directors will call in actors who don't have demos in special cases. Here are the reasons an actor will get called in to read.

Cynthia Songe: "They are very talented, can deliver, can take chances. Usually I have met them in my class or I have done their demo."

Actors often audition for parts that they aren't quite right for, yet if they impress the casting director, this often leads to another audition.

Cynthia Songe: "Yes, we call people back if they are good actors and right for other roles. The traits for an actor to be called back again are talent, creativity, and the ability to take direction. Someone would not be invited to future auditions because they just can't deliver the goods, they're not believable, or they sound like they're reading.

"Traits: talent and, yes, authenticity, believability, the ability to take direction, be fluid and flexible, creative, trust and offer up their own instincts."

How Do Actors Gain Success in Animation?

Animation is a fun and competitive side of voice-over. Here's some good advice about doing it well.

Cynthia Songe: "Many people think that it's about having funny voices. The voice talent and range is a wonderful quality and talent. But I cast characters . . . some real, some cartoon-y, but all, you guessed it, authentic and believable. Characters with personalities and size and dimension and feelings . . . not funny voices."

Bob Bergen: "Daws [Butler] taught me it's all about the acting!!! We worked from his original scripts, which were more like radio drama than cartoons. He stressed acting, timing, and character. Daws never even spent time on how to do voices. His approach was if your acting choices work the voice is bound to also be there.

"I can do Porky in my sleep . . . If you do a sound or voice that hurts never do it again! . . . The audition is five to ten lines. The cartoon, if for TV, is a four-hour session. If you lose your voice before the first hour is up you've blown this gig, your relationship with the director, etc. . . . "You can't rely on impressions of classic cartoon characters and celebrities. It's vital to be able to create original characters. I'm also a big fan of improv. Being able to give a character that li'l sumpthin' extra in the audition will nail you the gig. Improv skills come in handy there!"

What's Unique about Promos?

Marilyn McAleer offers a unique perspective on promos. She was a creative director at HBO and now is with the Atlas Talent Agency.

"Most VO talent isn't aware of the strategic difference between the two mediums (commercial and promo). Promos are much higher in energy and have a basic formula you need to follow. Commercials are more conversational reads and have an acting base.

"For the voice of a network (i.e., a primary voice that's heard over and over) the voice must be signature, and in some way communicate the brand while still standing out in a world of many voices.

"There's no such thing as one perfect voice-over. Every network is looking for something different.

"The most commonly requested voice is the gravelly male voice and the smoky female voice, though they are not necessarily the ones that get booked because the best *readers* are chosen."

How Have New Technologies Changed the VO Field?

The Internet and MP3s have changed the playing field in voice-over. Here are some insights into this changing world.

Cynthia Songe: "Prior to Voicebank I could hold auditions and see, say, about forty-eight actors a day. A full week of casting could garner about 200–250 actors per opportunity. This sounds like a lot, but when I am casting nine or twelve characters, it's not. With Voicebank, I can give anywhere from 500 to 1,000 actors the opportunity. On one hand, the competition is stiffer, on the other, the opportunity is greater. . . ."

Terry Berland: "I do listen to every voice suggested to me by an agent of Voicebank. If the actor does not have their voice up on Voicebank, they are at a disadvantage. I'll bring someone in whose voice I can hear over someone who has no sample listed with their agent.

"Because of the Internet and MP3s a client who is looking to cast non-union can reach all over the country to find the talent. They have access to talent in right to work states who are pretty good."

Wes Stevens: "More and more clients are recording from home. But that only makes sense if they are at such a level that they do not require direction. MP3s are fantastic and so is Voicebank. Our industry moves at a lightning pace these days. The field has been leveled to some extent."

Marilyn McAleer: "[MP3s] are efficient and effective when they [voice-over talent] nail it. They should expect to get calls asking for re-dos and be grateful that someone cares enough to shape their auditions rather than get annoyed and defend their choice of read."

Michael Maxwell: "We prefer to use AIFF files for broadcast, but if you are referring to the Internet, it's fantastic and offered nothing but opportunity for those who are willing to embrace the opportunities it offers."

There seemed to be a consensus that agents and casting directors don't have time to socialize with voice-over talent. They are much too busy doing their own jobs.

What Can an Actor Do to Improve His Odds of Success?

Finally, everybody gave simple tips for voice-over talent to succeed.

Marilyn McAleer: "They can practice and listen to their own reads; gain mileage to polish their abilities. They can listen to promo reads on different networks and brands and identify what they're missing to win those auditions. Few voice-over actors can define those differences and match them to their own skills."

Bob Bergen: "If you can take a piece of copy, spend very little time with it, and make it your own . . . give it a competitive read with a little something extra that makes you stand out, then you have that *something special.*"

Cynthia Songe: "Read a lot. Don't wait for auditions. Read and read and read, giving the illusion that you are not reading. Find as many acting beats as you can, and then throw it all out and re-direct yourself another way. Stay fluid and creative."

Terry Berland: "Never look to sell . . . Enjoy, study, and have patience."

It's important to always stretch your talents when you audition. Cynthia Songe elaborates this point. "Perhaps not getting pigeonholed . . . a.k.a., too typecast. As actors, we must make sure that through our demos and our reads that we show our range."

Cynthia also gives proper etiquette tips for voice-over talent to follow with agents and casting directors. "Keep it simple and professional. Arrive at an audition early to prepare for copy. Be polite. Allow extra time in case the auditioning is running late as they frequently do (often in order to give actors extra reads). Don't be afraid to ask questions about the copy if you don't understand it or if you don't quite understand the direction being given."

How Much Follow-up Should an Actor Do with Agents?

You can't get an agent without sending reels, but when is it too much or too little?

Cynthia Songe: "Inventory in agencies is usually in a state of flux . . . so that they (voice-over talent) may not get signed on one mailing or interview, but three to six months down the line their roster might have changed and the need might be there. Too much? . . . monthly."

Wes Stevens: "Once a year is enough to any given agent. If I get a reel more than twice a year, it looks desperate and it is doubtful that my signing needs and criteria have changed. Ultimately, get a referral; it is the most effective way to gain entry. Just submitting unsolicited is almost futile."

Do VO Actors Have to Live in Los Angeles?

Making the leap from a regional market to a national one takes good planning. Advice here can help you make a smooth transition.

Cynthia Songe: "Submit a demo to the agent and be available to either come to L.A. or audition via MP3 and if booked, do the spot via phone patch in their area or an ISDN line of their own."

Wes Stevens: "Move here. Literally. It is very difficult to work from outside the market. Even the *great* voices outside of L.A. have a hard time. New York. Chicago. Los Angeles. Get to one of those cities or be there for some stretch of time throughout the year."

Selena Smith describes the kind of talent that breaks away from the regional market and books nationally. "They are forward-thinking, career-minded people with a terrific business sense. They understand each market and the needs of clients. These people seem to understand marketing and advertising trends. They make it easy for the agent to book them. They adapt and change to current trends."

Some Tips from Producer Michael Maxwell

If you want to audition from home, says producer Michael Maxwell, "Proximity to the mic is probably the only concern, and a quiet environment."

You don't need to spend an outrageous amount on a mic for your home studio, either. "Anything above $150 usually sounds acceptable," says Michael.

Speaking about what he likes to see in the talent, when he is running a recording session he offered: "Enthusiasm, an ability to take direction, patience with confusing instructions from clients. Clean clothes and sobriety on the session."

Maxwell's father was a voice-over artist. Maxwell has a great inspirational story of how his father succeeded in the business.

"My father got into radio at thirteen years of age because his father was a janitor at the building in Detroit that had WWJ. . . . (He had a deep rich voice at a young age because of some respiratory illnesses he encountered as a child.) It was a new medium and they needed talent. He was approached in the lobby, and by the time he was fifteen, he was making more than his father and continued as a successful voice and on-camera actor into his seventies.

"He always worked. He got into commercials from his TV emcee and disc jockey jobs in Detroit. When he started, commercials were cut live, with a band, singers, and voice-over all in the same studio. At the time, having celebrities represent products with their voice was not usually the thing to do, so the market was wide open for actors who could take direction and had a good voice (usually deep).

"My father loved people and being in front of the microphone. It's what he lived for, and in a session, demo, or final, people felt it and responded to it. He could emote warmth and sincerity about anything, he had impeccable timing."

8

Welcome to the Games— Agents and Going Pro

What is an agent? Basically an agent is your sales representative. Agents get you auditions, but you have to book the job to get work. Many novice actors don't realize that agents don't get you work; you earn the work. Los Angeles agent Mike Soliday of Solid Talent says it best.

Mike Soliday: "If you get an audition and don't book the job, don't look any further than the person you see in the mirror. It's your job, the actor, to book the job! A lot of people think that jumping from one agent to another is going to make a difference."

You don't pay an agent any fee but they will make a ten percent commission off the jobs you book. Therefore, you need to prove to an agent that you can book jobs and sustain a career. This is easier to do if you've found jobs on your own or have a successful acting career. The only other way to be attractive to an agent is to have a compelling demo that truly reflects your skills.

What Does an Agent Do for You?

Have you ever had to look for a job? If you answer yes, then you know that's the hardest work in the world. In essence, that is what an agent does every day for their clients. They work so hard and you need to appreciate their efforts.

Mike Soliday: "The number of daily auditions varies—generally around eight to twelve a day. Currently, all of my auditions are done via the Internet and the talent's home studios. We get auditions through every possible channel. Subscriber based 'breakdown' services, Voicebank or other Web site providers, dealing directly with ad agencies, PR firms, Internet marketing companies, etc."

So an agent has to search for as many auditions as possible and either record all their talent or send the auditions via e-mail to their voice actors. Once that is done, they have to submit the completed MP3 files to meet the vendor's deadlines. That's a very full day!

Aside from getting all these auditions, agents also try to understand your unique talents so they can get you as many auditions as possible. Casting directors on the other hand, may only be interested in specific types you can fill for their audition specs. They have to find the perfect performer to please their clients.

Mike Soliday: "Yes, (generally) agents are more aware of 'their' talent's abilities. Agents help develop the actor's abilities. They have more direct interaction with the actor and therefore have a far deeper understanding of the actor's talents."

A casting director is very selective about the actors they audition, but an agent benefits from having as many working actors as possible on their roster. So there is a chance you'll compete for the same job with actors in your talent agency.

Mike Soliday: "You have to make sure you do have a couple of similar voices, especially if that 'style' is hot. An agent should have three guys who sound the same and all working as opposed to just one guy working."

How Do You Get an Agent?

If you interviewed every voice actor in SAG, you'd probably hear a lot of different ways actors secured representation.

Mike Soliday: "There is no magic formula for getting an agent. You need to cover all your bases. Submit demos, go to parties, network, ask friends to introduce you, etc. . . . Try every possible way. . . . And then try some more."

I concur with the aforementioned quote. I've used a variety of methods to obtain an agent. The most effective way to at least get a response from an agent is to have a mutual contact. However, there is no guarantee the agent will have room for you on their talent roster or that your skills will be on the same level as their voice actors. The best time to get an agent is when an agency has had a shake-up. In this case, a new agent may be coming in looking to make a fresh start. If you don't have any contact names to use when you send a demo then write a strong letter. Obviously, if you have an e-mail address you'll send an MP3 or a link to your Web site. Sell yourself on the jobs you've recorded, or theatre and film work you've done. Then call back to make sure the demo was received. You can leave a voice mail at night so you don't disturb the agent.

The best time to reach an agent directly is when their assistant is gone. This may be early morning, at lunchtime, or late in the day. My voice-over coach Wendy Dillon always said to have a mirror handy when calling to make sure you have confidence and smile. If you reach the agent, simply say that you sent your demo and wanted to make sure they received it and that you'd love to meet with them. Be prepared for any response, and respond politely. If they scream that they are too busy, simply say you are sorry and you know how hard an agent works.

You can find agents listed in *Ross Reports* for New York and L.A. and *The Voice-Over Resource Guide* is a must in L.A. SAG and AFTRA also have lists of franchised agents.

You can also use a search engine on the Internet to find talent agents in your area. Your reel will most likely attract attention with agents if you have an industry referral. In Los Angeles, I find it's even better if you can have someone affiliated with the agency *walk* the reel in to the agency.

Sound impossible? Well, I have gotten an agent before in New York by mailing in a CD. If this is your only chance, then do it well. Write a letter that will wow them. Emphasize your work, or that you have just booked a job. Mention union affiliations or related acting work. *Make sure your CD graphics are state of the art. Put your CD in a memorable package.* Make a follow-up call with the receptionist. When I moved to Los Angeles, I sent some headshots via priority mail to an on-camera agent. I think it is one of the reasons I got an agent instantly.

Making It to the Finish Line

I have found that persistence and patience are important if you are going to send out demos cold without a contact. For example, I was determined to get an agent and sent demos to every viable agency in New York City. I might have sent twenty or thirty reels in this instance. At the same time, I tried to learn all I could about each agency so I'd be ready for an interview.

I simply wrote a letter saying I was seeking new representation (this suggests that you have representation). I mentioned that I was the voice of Lifetime's Billboards. Then I said I'd love to meet with them at their convenience. Finally, I thanked them for their time. About a week after I sent the letters, I called each agency and asked if they had received my demo.

The responses from the agencies included: "We're not taking new talent, call back in three months; don't call us, we'll call you; and yes I'll listen and get back to you."

The Semi-Finals—An Interview

Finally, I got a call to go in for an interview. I must confess, I had an eye-opening experience the night before when I read a small booklet about agents, which I picked up at the drama store. This basically demystified the agent for me. It painted a portrait of person who works so hard for their clients all day. They make calls, do auditions, and have to pay for their overhead until they get a commission from a client.

It also stressed that an agent works for you, not the other way around. Therefore, you want to find someone who doesn't embarrass you or is unprofessional in any way. In other words, would you want an agent who promises more than they can deliver? The answer is probably not; they'll send you on auditions you can't do.

The agent/actor relationship is an alliance. You work together so it's important to feel comfortable with this person. In addition, you need to demonstrate to them that you are professional when you are interviewed. Be strong. Be articulate. Be confident. Be yourself.

Remember, too, that you are interviewing the agent to work for you. Have patience to wait for the right one. Trust your gut instincts. That's what I did when I went to my interview and established a great working relationship.

You should know that in some cities like New York, you may freelance with different agencies rather than being signed to just one agent. This is great when you are starting out. On the other hand, when you do get a contract, you should know that there is usually a renewal option for the agency. Therefore, if the agency feels you aren't booking enough jobs to justify the work, they may not renew your contract.

Win the Race for Work

Don't let the pressure to book ruin your audition. I remember I felt so much pressure to book with one of my agents that, of course, I never did. I just wasn't playing the game. Instead of focusing on the scene, I was pushing and tense. On the other hand, when I got my first audition with a New York voice-over agent I only focused on my acting, and I booked a job. It was a six-page industrial for Volvo. I read opposite the late actor J.T. Walsh. You absolutely must be playful and creative to be successful in the booth.

Once you get an agent and go out on auditions, you also must always be professional. Show up at auditions with plenty of prep time because you're new. If you can't make an audition, call your agent right away. I was shocked to learn that some voice actors don't show up for auditions! An agent can't sell your services to clients if you're not ready to play the game.

Also, don't rest on your laurels once you get an agent. Continue to market your demo. Always send thank you notes to clients when you work with them. Study continuously and practice at home.

Share Your Wealth

Send little gifts to your clients and agent on holidays. These may include small Godiva gift boxes, movie tickets, and gift certificates. For example, I sent Coldstone Ice Cream gift certificates to my agents for the Fourth of July holiday. Be creative. It's the thought that counts. Gift giving is a common industry tradition for actors. I can tell you that in the booming economies when voice actors have done well I have received gifts from Tiffany's when I was a writer/producer. A nice gift basket for a whole department is a great way to show your appreciation and not leave anyone out. If you bake, then bring in cookies.

Finally, always stay in touch with your agents but don't bug them for work. Let them know that you are working on improving your craft with classes. Keep them in the loop if you ever have a question about a job or contract. Have fun with every opportunity and you're bound to book jobs.

Run Ahead of the Pack with a Regional Agent

If you are in a large, highly competitive market, you may be able to find a regional agent in a smaller market. You will need to be able to send MP3 auditions to their office. Agent Selena Smith has great advice about the process.

Selena Smith: "Regional agent? Do your homework. Check the ad report to see what the hot markets are. Cincinnati, Pittsburgh, Chicago, Tampa. Send an e-mail with an MP3 to the agents. Check *www.AFTRA.com* for the list. Tell the agent why you should take a spot on their roster.

The most important thing: follow up. They are more important to you than you are to them. Agents don't have time to return phone calls—send something in the mail. E-mail, e-mail, e-mail!"

As always, try to think of places where you may have contacts. If not then send the demo just as you would for an agent in your area. Remember agents hear demos all the time, so you'd better impress them!

Just remember if you want to compete in a regional market then you must study the voice demos of the talent agencies. Go to the Web sites and listen to the talent roster if at all possible. You'll get a good idea how your reel compares to the signed clients.

Sell Yourself

It's important to study sales techniques because you are producing a product and service. Be creative in convincing an agent that they can't do without you. I learned this even more when we started receiving tapes for Emmy consideration after my husband won a Primetime Emmy Award. Networks really go to great lengths to create clever packaging to win votes. Approach your packaging as if you are competing for an award, too.

Needless to say, you should not rush the process. If you get no results, you should wait at least six months. Of course, you've got to repackage and update your demo so they hopefully forget what was sent before.

Slam Dunk

What do you do well?

Constantly re-evaluate where you are. As you study and progress, you will acquire new skills and tricks of the trade. Stop and just listen again to TV and radio spots. Is there something new you could add to your voice-over work?

Pick different times of the year to re-evaluate. Set up goals, change your workouts, and plan to meet new people in different parts of the industry. Say to yourself, tomorrow, I will learn more. For example, you can plan semi-annual progress reports for yourself to re-evaluate your work. Always have something to look forward to in your game plan. It's important to forget those auditions you didn't book and see endless possibilities ahead.

Always have someone in your corner, even if they are imaginary. Draw upon all the people in your life who said you could do it. Remember their key phrases. Make a list, write them down if you have to. Don't blow things out of proportion. On one audition I thought I performed poorly but learned later from the producer that I did a good job. The production just went in a different direction and they hired another voice actor.

There will be another job, audition, or chance. Too often we put too much pressure on ourselves. Some of the most successful actors had heartbreaking setbacks that led them to success. I honestly think the ebb and flow of ups and downs keep us sharp. It's like life. If we were all on one plane, it would be boring; like the monotonous black and white of the town in the film *Pleasantville*, it would be unbearable.

Study stars, athletes, and famous people you admire. Find out how they did it. Draw on their tenacity to feed your own success. On the other hand, aside from a professional setting, know when you need a break and take it. Don't be too hard on yourself. Having a little distance can bring you closer to the goal line.

Smile—force it, come on, you can do it. Ah yes, *breathe*. It's the little things that can help in a tense situation. Sandy Dennis said, "Sometimes you have to push it." Yes, indeed you just may have to push it a bit on a bad day. Always prepare a script two or three radically different ways prior to getting into the booth. If there is time and you're given a new direction, just say "*cool*" and go.

Whatever you decide, you'll need to create a strong home workout. Read ads, books, comic strips, and pick up dialects. Watch everyday scenes and listen for new sounds on the radio and TV.

Keep in the loop of local communication and create a voice-over workout group. Get a group of people together and just split the studio costs. In this case you will work together to give constructive criticisms to each other. It's a great way to find out what is happening and you'll be at a studio where engineers hear information from clients.

You always need to set career goals. Consistently re-evaluate where you are at and where you want to compete in the industry. Be realistic so you won't give up. Use friends as your support group and to build a grapevine. Finally, if you want to do voice-overs, have talent, and believe you can, you will.

In the end, if you're going to play the field of all voice-over work you need to be at your top fighting weight, so to speak. Like a top athlete, you must practice and practice to be ready to face any challenge. If you're ever in doubt, just breathe and imagine you're having a real conversation with someone you know. You're not alone as long as you imagine hearing them prompt you to say your lines. Then just jump into your scene with your *who, what, where* model and be free.

So now you've got the ball run—with it. Go out and win the voice-over game. Enjoy the whole process from acting to marketing. You can do it. But most important, when it is game time, play and have fun.

Personal Training Workout

▸ *Expand your studies.* Take acting, improv, or voice-over classes. Read for the blind. Find friends who are producers, agents, or people who have recording equipment. Respond to ads for jobs on the Internet (such as Craig's List or *www.entertainmentcareers.net*) or in the trades (*Back Stage*). Do play readings. Check out local radio stations. Decide what's best to take your act out and try your wings.

▸ Do an ice-cold read and see how you do. Listen to your work. *What are your strengths and weaknesses?* Work on improving your weak points.

▸ *Develop a strong home workout at least thirty minutes a day, five days a week. Network, breathe, and have fun exploring all you've learned.*

▸ Find a studio where you can record a spot. *Learn how to be a pro by doing it in a professional setting.*

· · · · · · · · · · · · · · · ·

Key Web Sites: *www.janetwilcox.com*

My Favorite Voice-Over Artists: Everyone on TV and radio who is working!

· · · · · · · · · · · · · · · ·

Appendix I

Legal Disclaimers

Valid Coupon
Offer good until December 31, 2020. Void where prohibited. You must have valid coupon to win. (:05)

Fresh Court
Offer is good only at participating Fresh Court stores, while supplies last. Sale ends July 9, 2020. (:05)

Wow Mart
This sale is for a limited time. Offer good only with coupon in participating Wow Marts until October 15, 2020. Void in Michigan, Ohio, and the Virgin Islands. (:10)

Study Points
Try timing yourself to see if you can work up to the times listed above. Record your work and listen back to see if you can understand everything. Start out slowly so your brain can take in the information. Also make sure you have a reason why you are telling it to an imagined scene partner.

For example, you may have to tell the person this information quickly because they are running out the door. This is isn't just about reading in a certain amount of time—you must imagine you are speaking to a real person, for a justified reason.

Promo Scripts: Study Points

Some networks may have a sole voice-over artist deliver all of the copy. This was the case when I was a writer/producer for The History Channel. Really think about the *product* when you work on the copy. If it's about history, you can create a character who may be a history buff, a writer, or an historian, for example. Make sure that you are telling this to one person when you deliver the copy. The reads should be friendly with a sense of storytelling or authority where appropriate. *Keep it conversational and avoid an announcer-y read.* When there is one voice for a network, the genres will dictate the flavor of the read. This demonstrates how a voice-over artist's range comes to play.

Usually detailed directions are given when voice-over artists audition to be the voice of an entire network. On the other hand, at HBO we usually brought in the talent we considered to be appropriate for specific campaigns. In this case, we would listen to reels, take suggestions from colleagues, or follow the dictates of our superiors in hiring talent.

Therefore, really let yourself have fun with the HBO genres. Think of the category of show you are promoting and how you would use your voice to pull it off. For example, a *Real Sex* spot may be raspy or sexy and playful. In contrast, a boxing spot would have energy and excitement. Just keep in mind that you still want to say it to one friend rather than going with an old time announcer style. You do talk with your friends about sports.

The copy includes a range of writers, so you'll have to adapt to different styles. Take your time with this copy. Study the voice-over styles on the air to get a feel for the different nuances. Find your niche and stretch to reach for the styles that are most difficult for you.

Script Formats

The layout for professional scripts varies for each writer. The promo scripts in this section are professional samples of the same format you would read, except of course normally the scripts would be on a regular size sheet of paper. There are some common traits for both advertising and promotion copy. Often there is a column for the visuals and for the audio. The audio will include information about sound effects and sound bites.

Sometimes there will be time code numbers to indicate the shots that will be included. You may have tags successively listed; you can do them all in a row. Just make sure to read them with the same energy level. Please note that you only read the voice-over parts, not the sections marked as *T/U*. The voice-over will usually be indicated as VO, announcer, AVO, or it will be set off in a different style of type. There may be other notations for things that are to be determined (tbd) or for the graphics (gfx). Remember to review everything in a script so you get an idea of what's on the screen.

There is no guarantee there will be visual descriptions, however. Some scripts simply have the words and you need to imagine what is on the screen. Pay attention to the style of the layout and get a sense of the piece. However, don't let punctuation or the script layouts trap you into a read that doesn't flow freely.

....

Promo Copy

Russia: Land of the Tsars
Run by lunatics, a genius,
      and a harlot :30

A global premiere event . . .

It was the largest nation in the world . . .

Run by lunatics, a genius, and a harlot.

The Tsars ruled over a people for

900 years of torture, murder and war.

Ivan . . . Peter . . . Catherine . . .

and Nicholas

This Memorial Day feel what life was

like under the most treacherous rulers

in the world.

Russia Land of the Tsars begins Monday

night, May 26th at 9 only on The History

Channel

A story so incredible . . . it can only

be true.

....

Promo Copy

Russia: Land of the Tsars
The Word Everyone Feared
:30

VIDEO	AUDIO
	A world premiere event . . .
	In a bold and reckless nation the one word everyone feared . . .
	TSAR
	Ivan . . . Peter . . . Catherine . . . and Nicholas
	This Memorial Day feel what life was like under the most treacherous rulers in the world.
	Russia Land of the Tsars begins Monday May 26th at 9 P.M. only on The History Channel.
	A story so incredible . . . it can only be true.

Promo Copy

Television Script

Client/Job Number: The History Channel   Version: 3.0

Product: Remember the Alamo

Title/Length: Dennis Quaid Promos

ISCI Code:
"ONE-SIDED" :30

	Dennis Quaid on the set of "The Alamo"
Dennis Quaid:	**On March 6, 1836, the Battle of the Alamo was a total massacre.**
	But the story of what actually happened here isn't so one-sided.
	Dennis Quaid stands near a cannon-blasted stone wall
	Now, The History Channel tells the Alamo story from both sides of this wall.
	Montage of clips from documentary
ANNCR VO/Super:	**"Remember the Alamo" Premieres Sunday at 9 P.M., 8 central only on The History Channel**
Dennis Quaid:	**The truth was also massacred that day.**

★★Note You Only Read VO Part . . . But It Still Must Have Energy!

Promo Copy

Television Script
April 1865
:30

> Our president was gone. . . . Generals were in rebellion
>
> In thirty days we would cease to exist as a nation
>
> But a handshake and one man's word changed history forever
>
> These are the 30 days that defined
>
> The 30 days that nearly ended us
>
> It wasn't a month, it was a miracle
>
> April 1865
>
> Monday April 14th at 9 P.M. only on The History Channel

Promo Copy

History Matters
"Moment"
:30

WHEN WE REACH OUT TO OUR PAST,

WE SEE HOW EVERY MOMENT IS CONNECTED . . .

. . . AND CAN BETTER UNDERSTAND THE WORLD
WE LIVE IN . . .

. . . THAT'S WHY—*HISTORY MATTERS*

THE HISTORY CHANNEL.

BECAUSE TODAY IS BUILT ON YESTERDAY.

Project: Real Sex 30

Version: Promo

Date: June 12, 2002

VIDEO	AUDIO
(gfx)	VO: A REAL SEX GUIDE TO MAKING GOOD SEX . . . GRRREAT!
(gfx) Trapeze artist flips to reveal red pasties	(VO) LESSON ONE—PUT A NEW SPIN ON AN OLD ROUTINE . . .
	T/U—BEING TOGETHER 17 YEARS, YOU HAVE TO FIND NEW WAYS TO HAVE SEX WITH EACH OTHER.
(gfx) and sex machine designer or woman's foot grasping machine	(VO) LESSON TWO— INVEST IN THE RIGHT EQUIPMENT . . .
	T/U—I THINK SEX MACHINE IS MADE FOR ME BECAUSE I LIKE GOING TILL I'M SATISFIED.
	Or
	T/U—BIG BALL HERE WILL HIT A G-SPOT JUST RIGHT

VIDEO	AUDIO
(gfx) and tightrope walker loses his pants, blushes	(VO) LESSON THREE— WEAR NOTHING BUT A SMILE . . .
From Fantasy segment, woman talks to camera	**T/U—I HOPE YOU'RE TAKING OFF YOUR CLOTHES WITH ME** . . .
From Circus segment	**Or**
	T/U—SHE'S NOT WEAR- ING ANY PANTIES
	(VO) IT'S AN ALL-NEW REAL SEX 30
	DOWN AND DIRTY
	PREMIERES AUGUST 3RD ON HBO
Woman leans head back into a harness	(VO) LEAN BACK AND ENJOY THE RIDE

Project: Southern Comfort
Version: Promo
Date: March 25, 2002

VIDEO	AUDIO
GRAPHIC OPEN	(V/O) ON THE NEXT AMERICA UNDERCOVER SUNDAYS . . .
As cowboy cleaning gun	(V/O) HE'S A GUN-TOTING COWBOY . . .
Pictures as little girl	BUT <u>HE</u> USED TO BE A <u>SHE</u> . . .
	(T/U—Robert & Lola) [Poor little boy being stuffed in drag . . .] that's my cross-dressing days.
Lola All dressed up	(V/O) SHE'S A BUSINES<u>SMAN</u> BY DAY AND A COUNTRY <u>GIRL</u> AT NIGHT
	(T/U—Lola) I've come out in a really big way . . . I'm like finding myself and all this and that.
	(V/O) THIS . . . IS NO ORDINARY ROMANCE . . .

VIDEO	AUDIO
	(T/U—Max) He was so shy. It took him a month before he would ask Lola out.
	(T/U—Robert) All the guys lust after Lola . . . I'm dating Lola. I haven't figured that one out yet.
Shots from show	(V/O) SOMETIMES, THE GIRL NEXT DOOR GROWS UP TO BE THE MAN OF YOUR DREAMS . . . (sot)
	(T/U—Lola) You're completely lovable.
	(V/O) AMERICA UNDER COVER SUNDAYS PRESENTS . . .
GRAPHIC CLOSE	(V/O) "SOUTHERN COMFORT"
	PREMIERES NEXT SUNDAY AT 10 ON HBO.
	PREMIERES SUNDAY AT 10 ON HBO
	PREMIERES TONIGHT AT 10 ON HBO
	COMING UP NEXT ON HBO.

Born Rich
They've got the world at their feet.

Not a bad view to wake up to . . . .

Platinum spoons in their mouths . . .

I grew up in [the] lap of luxury in New York.

Fistfuls of cold, hard cash . . . (cash register sounds)

It's not something I obsess about or think about.

And they've been told to keep it quiet.

—Money is a thing you don't talk about. It's in bad taste.

Until now . . .

I'd like to say that I'm reluctant to participate in this.

**An insider's guide to the super-wealthy . . . (cash register
sounds)**

(gfx. Directed by: Jamie Johnson)

(5 second gfx id montage)

Get the dirt on the filthy rich . . .

I don't feel bad for anything, especially having money.

Born Rich.

Premieres Monday October 27th on HBO (3.5 sec.)
Please note: The voice-over part is in bold type. The sound bites from the
show are in normal type.

The Gathering Storm Critics REVISED

Producer: Becca Schader 4/24/02
:40

VIDEO	AUDIO
HBO Films Logo into shot **GFX**: "an absolutely captivating film" *into* **GFX**: "rich, roaring" *into* **GFX**: "in-every-way stunning"	*Gavel hitting into* THE CRITICS HAVE PROCLAIMED *THE GATHERING STORM* IS AN ABSOLUTELY CAPTIVATING FILM . . . RICH, ROARING . . . IN EVERY WAY STUNNING.
	"Destiny commands, we must obey"
GFX: "the kind of movie they don't make any more, except now they have, and it's wonderful" —*The Washington Post*	**The kind of movie they don't make any more, except now they have, and it's wonderful**
GFX: "a prime candidate for television's movie of the season . . ."	A PRIME CANDIDATE FOR TELEVISION'S MOVIE OF THE SEASON
GFX: "Redgrave and Finney are a wonderful team to behold." —*The Orlando Sentinel*	REDGRAVE AND FINNEY ARE A WONDERFUL TEAM TO BEHOLD
Track up TBD	Track up TBD
Shots of Albert Finney **GFX**: "delivers sensationally, giving HBO another winner" —*Seattle Post–Intelligencer*	ALBERT FINNEY DELIVERS SENSATIONALLY . . .

VIDEO	AUDIO
GFX: "performance is not to be missed . . . V for victory." —*People Magazine*	HIS PERFORMANCE IS NOT TO BE MISSED . . . V FOR VICTORY.
The Gathering Storm	THE GATHERING STORM
GFX: SATURDAY 8PM/7 CENTRAL	Premieres Saturday Night at 8 on HBO
TONIGHT 8PM/7 CENTRAL	Premieres Tonight at 8 on HBO
THIS MONTH	This Month on HBO
NEXT	Coming Up Next ON HBO

©2002. Home Box Office, Inc.
All Rights Reserved.

CARNIVALE TEASE

THIS FALL . . .

HBO PRESENTS A NEW DRAMATIC SERIES . . .

GO INSIDE THE TENT AND DISCOVER THE MAGIC AND MYSTERY BEHIND THE NEW HBO ORIGINAL SERIES.

MAKING CARNIVALE . . .

PREMIERES SATURDAY AUGUST 21ST

©2005. Home Box Office, Inc.
All Rights Reserved.

Six Feet Under Catch Up Spot

Becca Schader
6/18/04

VIDEO	AUDIO
	LIFE'S TOO SHORT FOR REGRETS
	Track Up TBD
	IF YOU'VE MISSED ANY OF THE FIRST THREE EPISODES OF *SIX FEET UNDER* THIS SEASON . . . HERE'S YOUR SECOND CHANCE TO CATCH THE AWARD-WINNING SERIES.
	ON JULY 4TH, HBO UNEARTHS THIS SEASON'S FIRST THREE EPISODES.
	BACK-TO-BACK . . . ON ONE NIGHT.
	SUNDAY STARTING AT 8. TONIGHT STARTING AT 8
	COMING UP NEXT
	DON'T LET THIS SEASON FLASH BEFORE YOUR EYES.
	RELIVE THIS YEAR'S FIRST THREE EPISODES OF *SIX FEET UNDER* WHILE YOU CAN.

VIDEO	AUDIO
	DON'T MISS *SIX FEET UNDER* . . .
	TAGS:
	SUNDAY NIGHT STARTING AT 8 ON HBO
	TONIGHT STARTING AT 8 ON HBO
	COMING UP NEXT ON HBO.

Shock Video 2004: Too Hot for the Box

Becca Schader
Version 3
10/20/03

VIDEO	AUDIO
GFX: Holy hot box!	Holy hot box!
Monatge of People almost disrobing Candid Camera—Workout	IT'S titillating TV FROM AROUND the world.
Russian Big Brother	Woman: "Ohhh!"
Girl opens coat to reveal. . . . GFX: Pow! Camera travels down to under a table.	FROM THE SAUCY SLOPES OF SWITZERLAND. . . . TO THE LUSCIOUS LAND DOWN UNDER. . . .

VIDEO	AUDIO
GFX: Kapow! GFX: Thwack!	TANTALIZING TIDBITS THAT ARE JUST TOO TEMPTING!
Track Up from Naked News	Naked News: "You see where we're going with this?"
GFX: Twisted!	SHOCKING Series. . . . CARNAL Commercials. . . . AND RAUNCHY REALITY SHOWS THAT ARE TOTALLY. . . . TWISTED!
GFX: Bang!	Entertainment so hot. . . . IT'S EXPLOSIVE!
Title Page	The most <u>shocking</u> shock video EVER. . . . Shock Video 2004: Too Hot for the Box. . . .
Page with Jenna Jameson	NARRATED BY SEX SIREN JENNA JAMESON.
	COMING IN DECEMBER ON HBO. PREMIERES SATURDAY DEC 6 ON HBO. PREMIERES SATURDAY NIGHT AT 12:15 ON HBO PREMIERES TONIGHT AT 12:15 ON HBO COMING UP NEXT

World Championship Boxing "Combo" 4/03

Becca Schader
3/2/04

VIDEO	AUDIO
	THE HEAVYWEIGHT DIVISION IS UP FOR GRABS
Shot of Klitschko Brothers training powerful	AND THE KLITSCHKO BROTHERS EACH HAVE THEIR EYES ON THE PRIZE.
Gfx: April 24th Gfx: Wladimir Klitschko Gfx: Lamon Brewster Lamon Brewster footage	ON APRIL 10TH, WLADIMIR KLITSCHKO IS DETERMINED TO WREAK HAVOC IN THE HUNT FOR A HEAVYWEIGHT TITLE. . . . AS HE CLASHES WITH LIGHTNING FAST LAMON BREWSTER.
Gfx: April 24th Gfx: Vitali Klitschko Gfx: Corrie Sanders Corrie Sanders footage	THEN ON APRIL 24, HARD-HITTING, VITALI KLITSCHKO SEEKS REVENGE AGAINST THE MAN WHO BEAT HIS YOUNGER BROTHER— SOUTH AFRICAN SOUTH PAW, CORRIE SANDERS.
Shot of each Brother Shot of each Brother Shot of Two Brothers	TWO BOXING GIANTS TWO CHAMPIONSHIP DREAMS ONE CHANCE TO START WRITING HEAVYWEIGHT HISTORY.

VIDEO	AUDIO
Wladimir Klitschko—Lamon Brewster Saturday April 10 Saturday 9:45 pm/6:45 Pacific Tonight 9:45 pm/6:45 Pacific Vitali Klitschko—Corrie Sanders Saturday April 24th	LET THE NEXT ERA BEGIN ON HBO. . . .
Title Card Still Up	LIVE! SATURDAY APRIL 10

LIVE! SATURDAY NIGHT AT 9:45

LIVE! TONIGHT AT 9:45 |
| Gfx: BUILDING LEGENDS. . . . ONE ROUND AT A TIME. | BUILDING BIG LEGENDS. . . . ONE ROUND AT A TIME. |

STEP INTO THE NEW YEAR!

MAKE A RESOLUTION
TO LOSE THOSE EXTRA POUNDS. . . .
BROADEN YOUR HORIZONS. . . .
FORGET THAT EX. . . .
OR RECONNECT WITH OLD FRIENDS.

THIS NEW YEAR'S EVE, MAKE A DATE TO CATCH UP WITH THE GIRLS
IN BACK-TO-BACK EPISODES OF LAST SEASON'S *SEX AND THE CITY*.

ITS ALL LEADING UP TO THE FINAL EIGHT EPISODES
BEGINNING JANUARY 4TH.

TUNE IN WEDNESDAY, DECEMBER 31st. . . .
TUNE IN WEDNESDAY NIGHT STARTING AT 11. . . .
TUNE IN TONIGHT STARTING AT 11. . . .
TUNE IN TO SEX AND THE CITY, COMING UP NEXT.

THIS IS ONE RESOLUTION YOU'LL WANT TO KEEP.

PRODUCER: <u>ALBERTO FERRERAS</u>
PROJECT: *YOU'VE GOT MAIL*

WHEN I HEARD ABOUT *YOU'VE GOT MAIL*, I SAID.

MEG RYAN AGAIN???

TOM HANKS AGAIN???

IN A ROMANTIC COMEDY AGAIN??????

BUT THE TRUTH IS THAT ANYONE WHO HAS FALLEN
IN LOVE. . . .

AND IN HATE. . . . ON THE INTERNET. . . .

CAN RELATE TO IT!

SO I LAUGHED. . . .

I CRIED. . . .

AND I SAW IT AGAIN, AND AGAIN!

YOU'VE GOT MAIL!

This script has a very detailed list of visual shots and sound clips. The VO part you read is in bold on the left. Shots are listed on the right.

Sound bites from the movie and time code numbers are listed between the voice-over parts. Sound effects are listed as SFX.

SERVICE: **CINEMAX**	**DAT**	**AM**
PROD: **ALBERTO FERRERAS**	**TX**	**MUSIC**
ANOUNCER:	**EE**	
LENGTH:	**GRAFX**	
PROJECT: **STARRING CARY**		

GRANT

HIS NAME WAS ARCHIBALD LEACH. . . .

Holiday 01 03 46 *What?*

HE HAD THE LOOKS,
HE HAD THE CHIN,
HE HAD THE GIRLS!
. . . .BUT HIS NAME WAS ARCHIBALD LEACH!

Walk: 01 06 52 *Yes I suppose so.*

HE DID BLACK AND WHITE
HE DID TECHNICOLOR
HE DID CAPRA,
CUKOR,
HITCHCOCK. . . .

Arsenic: Holy Mackerel!

. . . .HE DID SOPHIA LOREN!

Houseboat SFX Slap

HE WAS FUNNY
ROMANTIC,
FATHERLY,

GRAFX

Holiday Flip.

Arsenic 01 19 56
Walk chin
Houseboat
Arsenic face

Arsenic face
Houseboat dance
Houseboat girl

**ATHLETIC,
HE KNEW HOW TO
CHARM YOU,
BUT LET ME REMIND
YOU. . . .**

Walk 01 04 43 Only if you must.

**. . . . THAT HIS NAME WAS
ARCHIBALD LEACH.**

Holiday: 01 03 05 Nooooo!

**JUST WHEN YOU THINK YOU
HAVE EVERYTHING, YOU'RE
STUCK WITH THAT NAME. . . .**

Houseboat
Why Should I Feel Guilty?

**ANYWAY, WE HAVE FOUR OF
HIS GREAT MOVIES, AND
THEY'RE RUNNING EVERY
SUNDAY AT NOON IN
DECEMBER, RIGHT HERE
ON CINEMAX.**

Holiday 01 22 29
That makes a lot of sense

**IT'S STARRING ARCHIBALD
LEACH, BETTER KNOWN
AS CARY GRANT.**

01 25 31

NICE GUY!

OR
Holiday: 01 10 10 Oh no!
Oh yes . . . .

BUT THAT NAME!

Holiday flips OR
Walk Marathon
Walk with Cigar
Holiday sofa with
Hepburn
Hepburn almost kiss
Holiday Flip

Houseboat wedding
Arsenic: Gagged

GRAFX TITLES
GRAFX TITLES

SERVICE: **CINEMAX**	DAT	AM
PROD: **ALBERTO FERRERAS**	TX	MUSIC
ANOUNCER:	EE	
LENGTH:	GRAFX	
PROJECT:		

FOR ME, <u>DOWN AND OUT IN BEVERLY HILLS</u> IS NOT ABOUT THE RICH GUY WITH A GUILT TRIP. . . .

Nolte jumping in the water
Dreyfuss jumping in the water!

01 05 54 Dreyfuss:
CALL 911, CALL 911!

HIS SNOTTY WIFE IS VERY FUNNY BUT IT'S NOT ABOUT HER EITHER. . . .

-01 04 11 WAKE UP
-02 18 02 Orgasm scene

01 16 42 Midler: That was the cherry on the cake of my day.

. . . . AND I REALLY DON'T THINK THAT IT'S ABOUT THE HOMELESS GUY WHO MOVES IN WITH THEM. . . . **EVEN THOUGH THAT DOG FOOD SCENE WAS PRETTY HYSTERICAL.**

01 51 07 eating dog food

02 21 34 There goes the neighborhood

FOR ME, THIS MOVIE IS ABOUT THE DOG.

Dog Barks.

02 51 30 BARKING

THAT CUTE, LITTLE LOVING PET NAMED MATISSE. . . .

01 34 06 Matisse loves no one

**JUST LOOK AT HIM!
I MEAN, THE POOCH
CAN ACT!**

01 50 02 Your dog thinks he's
human.

**HE'S AN ACTION HERO. . . .
HE'S GOT GREAT TIMING
FOR COMEDY. . . .
BUT HE'LL MAKE YOU CRY
WITH HIS STRUGGLE
WITH ANOREXIA.**

01 46 20 I believe he suffers
of nipple anxiety.

**I TELL YOU, THE MOVIE
IS ABOUT THE DOG!**

Ovation

THE REST IS JUST FILLER.

**PATHETIC HUMAN BEINGS
FIGHTING FOR THE LOVE
OF THIS EXCEPTIONAL
PUP.**

Nolte: I Agree.

**IF YOU DON'T BELIEVE
ME, CHECK OUT <u>DOWN
AND OUT IN BEVERLY
HILLS</u> AND TELL ME WHAT
YOU THINK!**

-02 13 49 Tai Chi
-01 35 12 rolling on his back

-covering eyes
-cookie sequence

-Charcoal run
-Frolicking

-Throwing food away

-jumping from trampoline

-The whole family looking
at Nolte.
Running around in the party,
jumping in the pool.

-Matisse Headturn

SERVICE: **CINEMAX**	DAT	AM
PROD: **ALBERTO FERRERAS**	TX	MUSIC
ANOUNCER:	EE	
LENGTH:	GRAFX	
PROJECT:		

ALL THE LETHAL WEAPON MOVIES ARE PRETTY GOOD....

Split screen in three

....BUT I THINK THAT THE SECOND ONE IS THE BEST ONE.

1. 01 03 50 MEL RUNNING
2. 02 46 40 DANNY ACTION
3. 01 00 17 TITLE FROM TRAILER

IT'S THE ONE WITH THE DRUG DEALERS FROM SOUTH AFRICA....

01 39 44 BAD GUYS WITH BOXES

01 39 44 MEL:
Hands up!

....WHO CAN'T BE TOUCHED FOR SOME POLITICAL THING....

SAME SCENE

02 49 15 BAD GUY
Diplomatic immunity

ANYWAY, IT HAS LOTS OF MEL OF COURSE, SOME DANNY AND SOME JOE

01 03 50 Mel Running
01 31 59 BOTH MAKE FACES
01 27 30 C/U JOE

01 29 57 PESCI
Can I please have some cotton balls for my nose

**IT HAS SHOOTOUTS AND
CAR CHASES**. . . . .

01 06 21 SFX: Car crash

A LITTLE ROMANCE. . . .
A LITTLE POETRY. . . .

01 58 12 MEL
Guys like you don't die in toilets.

**AND LOTS OF GREAT
ACTION SCENES**.

collage of action scenes

02 45 47 Mel fancy shooting
01 16 14 Car chase

02 16 19 ROMANCE
02 19 14 ROMANCE-SEX

01 38 41 Mel hanging from truck

01 28 25 BREAKING WINDOW
01 36 00 to
01 39 04 CRASH AND
SURFBOARD
01 59 41 SFX TOILET
ON CAR
02 08 10 SHOOT THE FISH
TANK
02 10 31 CAR DOOR
02 15 37 SWIMMING POOL
BOMB
02 16 57 HOUSE EXPLOSION
02 25 43 SHOOT NINJA
02 26 49 MEL HOOTS
HELICOPTER
02 32 20 HEAD THROUGH
WINDOW

01 31 30 PESCI
*Okay okay okay okay this is
the best part*

**ACTUALLY, THIS IS THE
BEST PART.**

01 32 49 Mel Topless
Hey Ross! Where does Trish
keep my laundry?

CAN WE SEE IT AGAIN?

01 32 49 Mel Topless
Hey Ross! Where does Trish keep
my laundry?

ONE MORE TIME!

01 32 49 Mel Topless
Hey Ross! Where does Trish keep
my laundry?

**HMMMMM! LETHAL
WEAPON 2.
I CAN SEE IT AGAIN AND
AGAIN.**

01 32 49 Mel Topless
Hey Ross! Where does Trish keep
my laundry?

TAGS

Commercial Scripts

The next section includes an array of commercial copy. Read over the specs
to establish your character and tone. Notice how different writers present
copy. You should think about the radio and TV mediums as you prepare.
Imagine what visuals and sounds would be used for TV, for example. Also,
think about the aural components of effects and music on a radio spot.

Please remember that you never read stage directions or do sound
effects. I've had students do that in classes. Usually it takes common sense
to figure this out. Just look for the voice-over or character parts. They are
usually clearly marked.

Commercial Copy Bensens

"The Big Spender"
:30 Radio (excluding local market tags)

SFX: Bensens at lunch

BENSENS' MAN: Hmm. . . . this burger is too good for a buck. I feel guilty, but hey I'm not sharing it! At a buck each I feel like I could have two. Yep who says there aren't any breaks for the *little guy*. I can even spare a *few* bucks. . . . Eh what the Heck!

"Hey guys it's on me!"

FRIEND: "On you?!"

BENSENS' MAN: You gotta love Bensens.

Specs

Gender: Male

Age: Late 20s to 40s

Tone: He should be confident but not too cocky. He's real but you can add a touch of character. Audiences should identify with him, therefore the character shouldn't be too broad or have an accent. He's an everyday working guy trying to make ends meet.

Study Points
Always read the entire script before you perform it. Try playing around with accents in your rehearsal if it helps you make a character choice, and then play it straight. If you are not in the age range see if you can sound right for the part without being too broad.

Sharps

"Getting Noticed"
:30 TV

Montage: Office Scenes ... cut to a party where Bill is a wallflower ...
Then to various office scenes with Bill ...

Annc: Bill wasn't someone you'd notice at the office. If it weren't for Bill's paycheck, no one would have known he existed. Then Bill shopped at Sharps.

Now Bill has two assistants to fight off a hoard of hungry admirers.

Sharps ... we're not ordinary and neither are you.

Cut to: Bill leads a conga line at the office.

Specs

Gender: Male or Female

Age: Late 20s to 50s

Tone: It should be conversational but with a deadpan tone. It's understated with a chuckle underneath. If you can pull off a parody of an *announcer type* and still get the humor—go for it.

Study Points
Really think of the visuals of the spot. See the character. He's the key to your read. Don't try to be funny. Play it straight. Remember the visuals will be a complementary element to the spot. Close your eyes and listen to your recordings as you visualize the scenes of the spot.

A special note: The *s* sound is an especially difficult tongue twister. I learned this as a writer/producer. Thereafter, I tried to avoid using this alliteration. However, as a voice-over artist you still should practice tongue twisters with this sound to be ready for any challenge.

Commercial Copy

Control
"Relief"
:30 TV

Annc:

If your tension headache is keeping you from your work, it's time to take control with Control. It's the only pain reliever easy on your stomach and good for the heart.

So go ahead—take Control and be in control.

(Fast Disclaimer)

Control is not for pregnant women, people with HIV, or liver problems. If you have more than two drinks a day, talk to your doctor before taking Control. Do not take more than the directed dose of Control. Stop taking Control immediately if you develop an allergic reaction (Cut to end of spot.)

Control. Isn't it time you took control of your life?

Specs

Gender: Male or Female

Age: Late 30s to 50s

Tone: It should be warm and natural. An air of authority is appropriate, but don't be aloof. It should be friendly and comforting but not sappy.

Study Points

What are the things that come to mind when you think of the product? For example: pleasure, sex appeal, relief, or satisfaction may be some things. What happens when you don't have the product? For example, loss of status, pain, or hunger may come to mind.

Remember to keep your character when you read the disclaimer. Don't let the direction to read it quickly distract your need to convey the information to your friend. Think of a real friend in need when you practice this copy.

XEROX COPIERS "MONK" 90:

ANCR VO:	(Monk working on manuscript) Ever since people have been recording information, there has been a need to duplicate it.
Father Superior:	(shows manuscript to Father) "Very nice work, Brother Dominic, very nice. Now, I would like 500 more sets."
Brother Dominic:	(mouthing words) "Five hundred more sets?!" (goes to friend at copy center) "Can you do a big job for me?"
ANCR VO:	(close up of copier at work) The Xerox 9200 Duplicating System is unlike anything we've ever made. It feeds and cycles originals. Has a computerized programmer that controls the entire system. Can duplicate, reduce, and assemble a virtually limitless number of complete sets—And does it all at the incredible rate of two pages a second.
Brother Dominic:	(finishes job in minutes) "Here are your sets, Father."
Father:	"Huh?"
Brother Dominic:	"The 500 sets you asked for. . ."
Father:	(Looks toward heaven) "It's a Miracle!"
	Super: XEROX

Gender: Male or female

Age: 30s to 50s

Tone: There is a tongue-in-cheek tone to this spot. The voice-over complements the scene so it can be warm and conversational. There can be a hint of reverence – but not over the top.

Study Point: Think of the voice-over as the setup and payoff for the scenes in this classic copy. The opening can have a bit of a documentary feel and then go into a more conversational style.

....

....

Burroughs Computers 30: TV (UNYSIS)

Ancr. VO:

Most people think of IBM before Burroughs.

Why not? They're bigger.

But bigger doesn't necessarily mean better.

Take, for example, small business computers.

The Burroughs B20 offers up to five times more memory and can store twice as much data as the comparable IBM computer. And our screen is 20 percent larger.

Any questions come up? Just pick up the phone and call our hotline.

You see, when it comes to choosing between IBM and Burroughs,

The question isn't who's bigger. It's who's better.

Gender: Male or Female

Age: 20s to 50s

Tone: An easy conversational feel with an authentic energy.

Study Points: You need to focus on the comparison here and the idea that quality matters. Remember to create a real conversation about something you believe is true.

....

Organ Donation 30: TV

Ancr VO:

Someone out there needs your help—and you've decided to save them.

Every year, thousands of people die waiting for organ transplants.

To be a donor, you must tell your family now,

So they can carry out your decision later.

Otherwise, it's like throwing a 12 foot rope to someone who's 15 feet away.

Organ Donation.

Share your life. Share your decision.

Gender: Male or Female

Age: 20s to 60s

Tone: Warm without being sappy.

Study Points: Focus on the setting where you would say this to a friend. Come up with heartfelt motivations to say this to someone.

Industrial and Marketing Copy

The next section includes two pieces of copy. The first script is for a company called *Healthology*.

You should go to the Web site and learn more about the company for clues. It is a fairly clear-cut genre. Medical reads have a definite tone and energy. This is a marketing tape to promote the company so it has more energy than the warm comforting tone of a straightforward medical script.

- *Gender*: Male or female.

- *Age*: Twenties to fifties.

- *Tone*: Upbeat but not perky. Friendly but hip. Avoid a heavy-handed authority feel.

The second piece of copy is for a Manhattan High School industrial. Use your imagination to come up with appropriate specs. Perform different styles and play them back. Decide what would work best for the copy. This is important because you may not get a lot of specs for industrial copy.

Study Points

Create a name for each character. Decide who you would say the copy to and for what important reason. Play around with putting yourself in different settings when you read it. For example, it might be at a business luncheon or a nighttime company event with a relaxed, happy feel.

....

Industrial Copy

Healthology is an award-winning health media producer of feature articles and video programming for distribution on the Web. Our unique blend of health professionals, seasoned television producers and cutting-edge technology informs and engages, capturing the attention of all audiences.

Healthology provides our distribution partners with a robust library of highly credible and highly produced educational multimedia health content for consumer audiences on a wide range of topics, with new content added every day . . .

GFX—General Wellness

Offering tips on staying healthy and preventing disease

GFX—Health Screening

Providing life-saving knowledge of screening tests

GFX—Personal Perspectives

Learning how others are coping with their illness

GFX—Treatment Options

Providing information to help choose the best treatment

With Healthology, the doctor is always in . . . delivering health information that empowers consumers to make knowledgeable

decisions about their health—content that will keep them coming back to your site.

(a) <u>Close</u>

Healthology, see what the leaders in multimedia health content can offer your users.

<u>ALT Close</u>
Healthology, see what the leaders in multimedia health content can do for you.

This Healthology script made available courtesy of Healthology, Inc. ©2006 Healthology, Inc. All rights reserved. Healthology logo are trademarks of Healthology, Inc.

....

....

Industrial Copy

Manhattan High School

There is a high school in Manhattan unlike any other. One that stimulates, excites, and challenges its students like few in the country. A school that raises the standard and takes a whole new approach to public education. Welcome to the High School of Economics & Finance.

Study Points
Although this copy is short, it still requires great energy and enthusiasm.

....

Multiple Character Study Points for Radio Spots

The next two scripts are examples of multiple character scripts for radio. Even if you're doing one part, read everything over including the announcer part because it usually sets up the scene or summarizes the concept of the spot.

You only record your lines. John Brosnan's script has many characters so you may want to highlight your part in yellow or circle your character name at the beginning of the line. Yellow is a good color for highlighting because it does the least damage if the type smears and it's easier to read. Find what works best for you. I have not given any direction for the characters because I think you can get everything you need from the script. It's also a good way for you to have to hunt for clues on your own.

....

Multiple Character Copy

Black Cow Classic Dip :30 Radio

ANNC: They were destined to meet . . . SFX: Polka music full up . . .

Two people bump into each other at a Polka contest.

Woman: Oh, excuse me!

Man: I'm sorry did I step on your foot?

Woman: Not at all.

Man: Do you polka much?

Woman: No, I just came for the dip.

Man: Dip? I didn't know the polka had a dip.

Woman laughs

Woman: No, I meant The Black Cow Classic Dip.

Man: Mmmm . . . I don't suppose you'd like a to-go cup for this?

Woman: Well what about your polka partner?

Man: I think I just met her.

Announcer: Black Cow . . . dip into something unexpected.

Polka music trails off . . .

Specs

Woman and Man Roles

Age: 30s to 50s

Tone: Real but maybe a little character. It's friendly but not too flirty until the end.

....

....

EXTRA CREDIT HOMEWORK FOR CLASS #9—JOHN BROSNAN COMMERCIAL COPY for "Mega Ultra Plus" by John Brosnan FINAL VERSION

DARRIN: Late 20s, the goofy king of the water cooler.

BOB: Early 50s, a smooth operator until his confidence was destroyed last night.

SUZY: Late 20s, wry and matter-of-fact (sort of) about Bob's "problem."

SOUTHERN ASTRONAUT: 30s, deep-South flyboy á la Chuck Yeager. Always heard over his helmet intercom.

ANNOUNCER: Sympathetic; macho; fast with the legal jargon.

DARRIN: Big Bob, how'd it go last night with Suzy from Accounting . . . ?

BOB: Well, uhhhh . . .

DARRIN: Are you blushing, Bobster? How unlike you . . . hey, here she comes . . . !!

BOB: Ooooh, noooo . . .

DARRIN: Hiya, Suzy! Lookin' good!

SUZY: Darrin. (pause) Good morning, Bob . . .

BOB: Uhhh, yeah, hi Susan. I mean Sue . . .

SUZY: You're up early, Bob. (whispers) Wish I could've said the same for last night . . .

BOB: Ugh . . .

ANNOUNCER: (sensitive) "It just wasn't meant to be . . ."; "Don't worry, it happens to all men . . ."; "We can try it again tomorrow . . ."

SFX: A BIG ROCKET STARTS UP

ANNOUNCER: Hey, men, have you ever had "issues" with lift off . . . ?

SFX: THE ROCKET PETERS OUT PATHETICALLY . . .

SOUTHERN ASTRONAUT: (filtered) Houston, we have a problem!

SFX: ROCKET RE-STARTS, THE RUMBLE BUILDS STEADILY . . .

ANNOUNCER: (macho) Then strap in cowboy, 'cause with Mega Ultra Plus, this rocket is goin' ta the Moon!!!

SOUTHERN ASTRONAUT: (filtered) Liftoff!!

SFX: THE ROCKET RISES POWERFULLY . . .

ANNOUNCER: Push the outside of the envelope with the male-enhancing formula that just won't quit!!

SFX: THE ROCKET ROARS PAST

SOUTHERN ASTRONAUT: (filtered) Woo-hoo! Houston, I am good for another ten orbits!!!

ANNOUNCER: With Mega Ultra Plus, the skies' the limit!!

SFX: THE ROCKET CONTINUES MIGHTILY ON ITS MISSION . . .

SOUTHERN ASTRONAUT: (filtered) . . . that was one giant step for MANkind! Houston, the Eagle . . . has . . . landed!

Specs

You're on your own with this script. Make your own choices.

....

Books and Character Copy

I have included a complete version of my children's story *A Boy Named Blue*, since it's short, and only an excerpt from *Fifi of Fifth Avenue*. The excerpt is more like a side for an audition. In this case, you have to use your imagination to fill in the missing details of the story. However, you can refer to the character breakdowns for some clues. Children's stories are wonderful because they lack the complexity of adult books. On the other hand, the characters can be broader so you can prepare for animated work.

You have the opportunity to do an entire audio book with *A Boy Named Blue*. You will read the title page and then say, "read by" and then say your name.

Whatever you do, don't assume a false tone as a narrator. You're still a character telling this story to one person. Be real and don't *talk down* to your listener.

Break the work down. Practice the narrator, then practice each different character. The character work is a good way to practice coming up with animated characters. Books have a slower pace than animation, however. Really study the work of narrators on audio books you get from the library. Compare this pace to the quicker delivery required for animated characters.

Finally, put everything together and read it all at once so that you move from the narrator to each character. *Work at your own pace. Only do what is comfortable for your voice and your current skills. You can always come back to it at another time when you've acquired more skills.*

A BOY NAMED BLUE, By Janet Wilcox

His name was Blue and he didn't know what to do because he was green with envy over Red. Red had such a bright name, so vibrant and bold. "*Blue,* what kind of a name is that," he said.

Yellow came by full of sunshine and good times and she said, "Oh, Blue, you must be true to your name or you'll never be the same." But Blue just cried because he had tried. "I'm just Blue and there is nothing I can do."

Green was passing by and couldn't help but spy. "Hello Blue, is it true you want a new name?" Green said with a spring in his step. "Yep!" Blue wailed, "I'm Blue! I'm just blah, blah, blah." "Ha," said Green. He always had a soothing touch and Blue liked him so much. "If my name was Red, people would like me, don't you see?" "No!" said Green and Yellow with glee, "We like you Blue, otherwise you wouldn't be you!"

Red chimed in too, "Yes that's true!" "Red!" Blue cried caught by surprise.

"You notice me," Blue sighed. "Of course I do," Red replied. "You make me feel calm and cool. I don't know what I'd do without you."

Then Red, Yellow, Blue, and Green played together all day and danced in the light and knew everybody was just right, because together they could make a beautiful rainbow. You can too, if you just let your true colors show!

Fifi of Fifth Avenue

Character Breakdown

Fifi – a beautiful young poodle aspiring to be a hero

Shawna – a shameless Sharpei who is Fifi's classmate

Trixie – a tireless Terrier who is Fifi's classmate

Rollo – a jaunty Jack Russell Terrier who is Fifi's classmate

Tianna – a tyrannical Poodle who is Fifi's classmate

Bonzo – a big-hearted Collie who is Fifi's classmate

Shakespeare – a sleek and sassy Afghan who is Fifi's classmate

Sean – Wilhemena Brandt's dog walker and an aspiring actor with a heavy brogue from Brooklyn

Brent – a lanky Labrador who saves Fifi's mother, Belinda, from a robber

Mrs. Pridilly – the principal of the dog charm school

Charlotte – a young girl who owns Fifi and wants more than Fifth Avenue wealth

Jerry – the German Shepherd guide dog

Will – Charlotte's father who is successful but doesn't give a hoot what other people think

Bruce – a big Bulldog in Central Park

Buela – Charlotte's caregiver, she is as big as any nanny, with a heart to match her girth

Belinda – Fifi's beautiful mother and Wilhemena's cherished dog

Alex – a bully from Charlotte's day camp

Charlie – Charlotte's new friend and protector

Officer Finnegan – the cop who nabbed the thief who tried to snatch Belinda's valuable necklace

Wilhemena Brandt – the eccentric aging actress who owns Fifi's mother and employs Sean

Katherine – Charlotte's mom who is stuffy but kind hearted deep down

Rob – a young Rookie cop

Fifi of Fifth Avenue—Excerpts

Graduation

Fifi's training was nearly completed, and it came time to share her hopes with her fellow classmates. Shawna very openly said she would use her training to get extra treats, while Tianna said she'd lure the finest looking dog to do her bidding. Shakespeare wanted to serve his master with the utmost class and intelligence, yet Trixie hoped to play all day. Bonzo wished to bring joy to the little boy he lived with and Rollo just hoped to sit still for a few minutes.

Then Fifi topped them all. "I want to be a hero I want to do good. I want to help people, even save people," she proclaimed. At that, Tianna and Shawna burst into laughter.

"Oh you must be joking dear," Shawna scoffed. "You, a hero? No, I don't think so." She added.

"How unladylike," Tianna chimed in. "For a dog of such breeding," she snickered. "Now, not so rough there," Shakespeare added. "It is a thing of good she wishes," he preached. "But a girl of such beauty dare not venture that way my dear," suggested Bonzo.

"You could get hurt," Trixie added.

Then Rollo jumped up and struck a play dead pose. "You can save me any day," he invited. Everyone laughed.

But Fifi was heartbroken. Ever since that day with her mother, Fifi wanted to do something like Brent had done—return the favor, maybe do something dogs were meant to do. It seemed so sad, because she wasn't a big dog or even that strong. Yet she yearned for it as the days went by.

Suddenly Fifi snapped out of her sad mood and decided to take action. All she had to do was learn how to be a hero. After all, she was practically the best student Mrs. Pridilly had ever seen.

So Fifi made a point to observe all the dogs she could. She was particularly interested in the German Shepherd, Jerry, who was a guide dog. She observed as he watched for the light to change and then nudged his master along. He never lost focus, he was always watching. "I must keep my ears and eyes open and pay attention," Fifi noted.

Then she came upon a dogfight in the offing. A silly little Pekingese was picking a fight with a great big Greyhound. Out of nowhere a woolly Sheep Dog appeared baring his teeth at both of them. "I must be tougher," Fifi vowed. She started to bare her teeth, but an onlooker just pointed out how pretty they were. "I got to work on that," Fifi thought.

Charlotte had no idea about Fifi's escapades. She was too busy going to birthday parties, participating in her class play, and begging her parents to send her to a coed camp. "Come on daddy! I'm with the girls all year. I want to play real sports and have fun," she campaigned.

Will smiled knowingly and added, "This doesn't have anything to do with a particular boy does it?"

"Oh sure daddy, like I even know any," she teased. "Come on pleeeeease."

"Oh, all right, but your mom won't like it." Charlotte frowned. "It's OK, leave it to me, I'll take care of everything," he said and winked. Charlotte hugged her father and ran to scoop Fifi into her arms.

"Did you hear that Fifi? I'm going off to summer camp with boys too!" Fifi yelped with approval.

But deep down Fifi smelled trouble. Suddenly she realized she had a keen sixth sense and this could come in handy for a hero, so she plotted to keep a close watch on Charlotte from now on.

Play Time

The grass grew greener and a heavy sweet scent hung in the air as Fifi frolicked about in Central Park. It was a wonderful summer day. Dogs flew freely across the lawns. Buela chatted on a park bench, as Fifi was lost in the canine games. Charlotte was off to camp so there was time to take it easy.

A big Bulldog, Bruce, tipped Fifi on the nose and said, "Hey baby how's about a walk in the park?"

"I'm afraid I must stay with my master," Fifi explained and turned to walk off.

"You stuck up little wimp, who needs you," he shouted. That stung quick to her heart and Fifi felt a tear well up in her eye. She dare not turn back, but her hurt feelings grew heavier with every step. She wanted so to break down into full sobs, but she kept walking.

Just in the nick of time a gentle voice assured, "it's all right, my dear!"

"Momma!" Fifi cried. And then like a river rushing in a flood, her tears sprang forth. "Oh momma, I'll never be a hero. No one takes me seriously. I'm like a pretty porcelain dog. No one sees that I have feelings. I have thoughts. I want to be more and I know I can—I just do." Fifi sighed.

"Ah, my dear, you're a beauty and that's a blessing. Your charms and wiles will win you many things. There's nothing wrong with being a lady," she consoled.

"But mom, I can do more. I know it," Fifi exclaimed. Then without warning, Fifi fell into a crying spell.

"Now, now my dear, life is long and life is short. It all depends on how you live it. The road gets rough or the ride is smooth. It's all in how you drive through it. You can set your sights so high you'll never see the sky. Or fix an eye so low you'll never know how to laugh and love and live your days to the fullest," she explained.

"But momma . . ."—(Belinda put her paw out and shushed).

"Sure you're bound to have days when you're feeling sad and lonely or maybe you're just true blue," she said.

"So what should I do," asked Fifi.

"Remember a little song my momma sang to me. It's called *A Moment Is A Memory In A Minute*," Belinda said as she raised her head to croon.

[Please note: The song is deleted.]

Fifi giggled, "Oh momma!" They hugged. But within moments, their happy reunion was torn apart. Little feet came running for the park. The children had arrived from camp. The dogs scattered away. Charlotte trailed behind running after the boys.

"Hey, let's play a game of football," Alex shouted.

"Yeah," the guys cheered and gathered for teams.

Charlotte stepped up to play.

"Wait, you're the only girl, we're not at camp anymore," Alex protested.

"So what," Charlotte shot back.

"Come on, guys, give her a break," Charlie yelled from the sidelines. He had just had surgery on his leg and was on crutches.

"Oh, you wanta' make something of it Charlie," Alex challenged.

"Wait a minute," Charlotte interrupted, "This isn't that big of a deal. What are you going to do—hit a guy on crutches?"

"You're right, I can start by keeping you out of the game," Alex insisted.

"Well, I'm playing," Charlotte said.

"OK," Alex scoffed and gave her a hard shove. She fell, Charlie ran forward and Fifi flew in to help. Yelping and yelping, she alerted Buela who dashed away from the bench. Dogs barked, children screamed, and Buela scolded. It was total chaos—until two black shoes appeared, topped by blue pants and a shiny badge.

A silence fell over everyone in the presence of Officer Finnegan. "You kids gotta' problem? Fine, work it out, but, Madam, don't leave your bag! There's been five purse snatchings in the past week. It's just not safe," he warned.

"Oh, thank you officer," Buela replied. "As for you children, behave! And there's no need to raise a fuss Fifi. I have eyes on my girl at all times," Buela insisted. "Now come along Charlotte."

Charlie reached down and gave Charlotte her baseball cap and Alex sneered while she walked off. Meanwhile Fifi was given glaring looks by Tianna and Shawna who had witnessed the whole scene. "A hero," Tianna scoffed.

Fifi's heart sank and would have drifted deeper if she hadn't run into Brent and Sean. "Ah Buela Fifi's lookin' so fine," Sean praised.

"Well we've had a bit of a mishap," Buela added.

"Oh, nothing to worry about," Sean insisted. "I wanted to give you a flyer. I'll be performing in the park," he announced.

"Oh, lovely," Buela gushed.

"Yes, it's Shakespeare's *A Midsummer Night's Dream*," Sean beamed with pride.

"How appropriate," Buela added. "We'll have to come, Charlotte."

"I'm playing Puck," Sean shouted off as they drifted apart.

Brent nodded to Fifi. "Very nice work, looking after your master. People don't always know a hero when they see one." Fifi blushed. It was the highest compliment she could have ever received. Fifi hummed her momma's tune as she saw Belinda walk off with Sean. He handed Wilhemena Brandt a flyer. Her grand Shakespearean gestures grew smaller as they approached home.

"Ah, what a day," Buela exclaimed as she tucked Charlotte into bed. Katherine came in to kiss Charlotte and saw the advertisement for the play.

"Shakespeare in the Park! We must go. I've heard everyone will be there opening night, and you Miss Charlotte will be the prettiest girl there," she whispered. Charlotte nodded and fell asleep as Fifi sighed.

Animation Copy: Study Points

The following section has two sample animation scripts that John Brosnan wrote. The first one, *Who's Got The Binky*, has all the fun charm of the *Family Guy* show with plenty of attitude from the Bronx.

Before you start, watch some cartoons and pay attention to the pacing. Mirror the line delivery and apply that rhythm to your work when you record this script. In other words, act and don't lag behind if your reading skills aren't ready. Rehearse the parts before you record so you really sound like you're in the scenes. Take a week to build up to it if you need that much time. There are plenty of characters to play with and you can shape your character with specific placement and dialect choices. Turn to Appendix IV to find the Web address for dialects.

I asked John to write these scripts because I think his characters are very clear and you don't need breakdowns. With this in mind, you can experiment with an adult style of voice for the babies. Draw on the character Stewie from the *Family Guy* for ideas (go to *www.familyguy.com*). When you read, just pick out one part you think you'd be likely to book, but also perform the whole script out loud for a stretch.

Play from the Heart

The second script, *Squirt Trek*, is more like Mel Brooks meets *Space Ghost* and *Futurama* (go to *www.adultswim.com*). The characters may give asides to the audience and they have pithy dialogue. Think about action-hero comic strips for this one. Although these characters are broad, please resist the temptation to *play at them*. In other words, believe you are the character and don't *comment* on your part. For example, make strong choices so you believe you are the Demsela (á la Madeline Kahn in *Young Frankenstein* perhaps).

Also, play against type. Record your performance, then listen back and decide which takes showcase credible characters with real heartfelt emotions.

Remember, comedy is very serious. Sometimes, I'd get the biggest laughs when I gave what I thought were my character's most serious lines in plays. For example, we laugh when someone falls on a banana peel. Misery is funny. When I studied with Paul Sills, he stressed that we should never try to be funny—we should just play the scene. Do the same with these animation scripts, don't fake it; unearth your unique vulnerabilities.

"WHO'S GOT THE BINKY?"

The scene is a nursery-type day care center packed with babies.

BABY ELROY
WAAAAAH! WAAAAH! WAAAAH!!!

The leader, an infant from the other side of the tracks, pipes up.

JOEY NAPS
Okay, listen up, diaper heads! What we got here is a red alert sort of situation: Baby Elroy is unhappy. And when Baby Elroy is unhappy, *I* am unhappy. And when I am unhappy I get a real nasty diaper rash.

OTHER BABIES
EEEEEW.

JOEY NAPS
Right. So, in order to maintain peace and order over here in the nursery, we gotta come up with one thing . . .

ROSIE LOPEZ, baby girl with a knack for hard knocks, crawls over.

ROSIE
A cookie?

JOEY
Nah.

SHEMP, less than a future MENSA candidate, pulls his thumb out of his mouth.

                    SHEMP
        Cake?

                    JOEY
        Nah–ah.

TRISHA, future debutante, as always, waits for a shot.

                    TRISHA
        Some class, perhaps?

                    JOEY
        Nah, none'a the above, you diaper dolts!
        We need ta find Baby Elroy's binky!!!

Baby Elroy continues to wail hysterically in the BG.

                    ALL
        Ohhhhhhh.

                    TRISHA
        How quaint.

Joey lets that one pass.

                    JOEY
        Now we gotta break up inta search parties.
        Shemp: you take the crib.

SFX Shemp starts to pull on a crib.

                    SHEMP
        Where do you want it, Joey Naps . . .?

                    JOEY
        Would ya drop it on my head? (sigh) Never mind.
        Trisha, you check under the . . .

She clears her throat obsequiously.

TRISHA

Mister . . . Naps, perhaps you missed the fact, but I will have you know that my Mah-ma drops me off each and every day in a BMW 380xxii to the third power.

(pause)

So as to this quaint little search party, I must decline. There are people who do this sort of thing . . .

Rosie rapidly crawls to her favorite spot: in Trisha's face.

ROSIE

Oh, don't get all lookin' at me, baby! I'm eleven months old and I WILL give you the spankin' yo "Mah-ma" NEVER gave you!!

TRISHA

Oh, REALLY!!

ROSIE

Yeah, whitebread. REALLY! You think you own the whole nursery Ms. Designer diapers . . . ?!

I'll be ALL over you like white on rice cereal!!

Baby Elroy continues his loud cry.

JOEY

Aw'right, knock it off already, will yuse?!!

I dunno what's worse: yuse two over heah jabbering or Baby Hell-roy beltin' it out like Caruso over there! I DO know one thing:

(pause)

WE GOTTA FIND THAT STINKIN' BINKY!!!

SHEMP

I want cheese.

JOEY

Don't we all . . . Oy, I'd rather be teething . . .

Baby Elroy cries and cries some more.

"SQUIRT TREK"

> ANNOUNCER
> We now return to our regular program, already in progress . . .

We know DAMSELA, the curvy blonde from a million horror movies.

> DAMSELA
> Help! Help!! Who will save us from this evil and vile alien menace . . . ?!!

We hear a HUGE and UNINTERESTED ALIEN MONSTER YAWN.

> DAMSELA
> It'll tear me to pieces! Somebody, for the love of Oz, please heeeeelp!

We hear giant footsteps as the ALIEN MONSTER inches closer to Damsela.

> MONSTER
> Oh, sorry, were you talking to me . . . ?

> DAMSELA
> Yes, you evil, nasty beast!

Monster looks around from side to side.

> MONSTER
> Huh. "Evil". . . ?! Uhhh, do you have the right . . . um, alien . . . ?
> (pause)
> And I don't see how I've been anything but nice . . .

> DAMSELA
> Yes, you hideous, wretched, foul . . .

MONSTER
Whoa-whoa-whoa, hold the phone . . .
(pause)
I cooked dinner . . .

DAMSELA
(continued)
—horrific, nightmarish—

MONSTER
Baked cookies.
(pause)
From scratch. Hello?

DAMSELA
(continued)
—horrid, slovenly, glutinous—

MONSTER
Cheap shot. I am big boned, thank you.

DAMSELA
(continued)
—dirty, disheveled, uncoordinated—

MONSTER
Oh! That's uncalled for! I happen to be color blind.
(pause)
And a skosh A-D-D, as if you cared.

DAMSELA
(continued)
—repellent, irksome, malodorous—

MONSTER
(pit check: sniff, sniff)
You're really starting to hurt my feelings now.

                    DAMSELA
              (continued)
        —diseased, disingenuous, jejune—

                    MONSTER
        Did you just insult me in French?!

                    DAMSELA
              (continued)
        —dour, dull, indiscreet—

                    MONSTER
        You don't want to see me angry. Not pretty.
              (pause)
        Trust me on this.

                    DAMSELA
              (continued)
        —dreadful, defunct, dung-like—

                    MONSTER
        There's a line. And you are about to cross it.

                    DAMSELA
              (continued)
        —curmudgeonly, crass, sub-par—

SFX: The Alien Monster flips through a Thesaurus.

                    MONSTER
        Is there anything left . . . ?

                    DAMSELA
              (continued)
        —vituperative, peripatetic—

                    MONSTER
        Great. Now we're using the S-A-T words . . .

Finally: silence. The Alien Monster lets out a long sigh.

MONSTER
(sincere)
Feel better?
(pause)
Can we talk . . . ?

DAMSELA
Somebody help me!

The Alien Monster sighs. In that instant, SPACE CAPTAIN SHANE V. BLERK, man of action and little thought, materializes.

BLERK
E gads!

MONSTER
Does anyone ever knock . . . ?

DAMSELA
I'm saved!
(pause/sarcastic)
It's about time . . .

BLERK
Stand behind me, oh shapely damsel in distress, for I shall protect you from this filthy alien beast.

MONSTER
Oh, great. Here we go with the trash talking.

SFX: Blerk unholsters his deadly de-stazer pistol.

BLERK
I warn you, vile beast! Stand back or I shall have to dematerialize your nauseating visage.

MONSTER
There's a new one. One word for the Captain: Botox! Works wonders with double chins . . .
(pause)

Look. I'm sorry. This is all a misunderstanding. I'm tee-ing off in the next quadrant in about 15 parsecs . . .
Can't we just shake claws like civilized beings, maybe grab a Tazo at Starbucks or something—

Damsela shrieks in horror.

> MONSTER
> (aside)
> Soooo glad I don't have ears. Whew.
> (pause)
> This is a bad scene. I'm just gonna motor and leave you two lovebirds—

> BLERK
> Stand back! You'll get no further warning, you unholy—!

SFX: ZZZZZZT! Blerk fires his pistol in a blaze of glory and sound effects. No being could survive such a fusillade. Long pause.

> MONSTER
> Are we done yet, tough guy? Feel this—
> (SFX: knock knock) . . .
> —I'm made of pure *indestructonium*, Captain Einstein!!

Damsela gasps.

> MONSTER
> Big man with a gun.
> (pause)
> Normally, I'd just fire a stream of hot lava from my eyes and incinerate you both, but the lava kind of gives me a migraine. That and my Shrink has got me on the whole inner child thing, so I'm gonna throw you a pass.
> (pause)
> Vaya con Dios, Captain and Tennille.

MONSTER
(continued)
Taxi!

SFX of a car door SLAMMING CLOSED.

MONSTER
(to CABBIE)
Get me ta planet Pismo and step on it!

SFX of the Taxi lifting of into space in quite a hurry.

BLERK
That poor, twisted . . .beast.

DAMSELA
(dreamy)
I wonder if he'll ever call me . . .

Appendix II

Read Styles

- Animated/Characters
- Announcer (Game Show)
- Announcer (Over the Top)
- Announcer (Promo)
- Announcer (Radio D.J.)
- Announcer (Sports)
- Arrogant
- Attitude
- Character-y
- Conversational
- Credible
- Deadpan
- Documentary Narrator
- Dry
- Flamboyant
- Friendly
- Gen-X
- Hip-cool
- Industrial/Corporate Narrator
- Laid back-cool
- Low key
- Man-on-the-Street
- Non-announcer

- Over-the-top

- Poignant

- Real/Natural

- Reflective

- Sad

- Sarcastic

- Sincere

- Smooth

- Storyteller

- Surfer

- Sweet

- Upbeat

- Wacky

- Warm

- Whiny

- Wry

*Reprinted courtesy of Voicebank

Appendix III

General Character Checklist

- Name:

- Occupation:

- Favorite—Food, TV Show, Song, Dance:

- Describe Where You Live:

- Married/Single:

- How Many Children/Siblings:

- Age:

- Republican/Democrat/Other:

- Fun Things You Do:

- Physical Activities:

- Hair Color:

- Body Type:

- Secret Desire/Character Vulnerability:

- Education:

- What Just Happened?

- What Do You Want Out of the Scene?

- Where Does Your Scene Take Place?

- What kinds of feelings do you have about your setting?

Appendix IV

Voice-Over Internet Links

- Voice-over and Agency Data Base
  - *www.voicebank.net*
- Care of the Voice
  - *http://choirsinger.com/sing.htm*
- Animation
  - *www.dawsbutler.com*
  - *www.bobbergen.com*
- Radio Scripts
  - *www.emilsher.com/radio/rivalry.htm*
- Tongue Twisters
  - *http://www.geocities.com/Athens/8136/tonguetwisters.html*
- Promo
  - *www.tvguide.com*
  - *http://www.promax.tv/main.asp*
- Commercials
  - *www.adweek.com*
  - *www.wheresspot.com*
- Dialects
  - *http://www.ku.edu/~idea/index2.html*
- Demos
  - *www.compostproductions.com*
  - *www.1042vo.com*
  - *www.blupka.com*

- Cartoons
  - *www.cartoonnetwork.com*
  - *www.nickelodeon.com*
- Voice-Over Job Listings
  - *www.craigslist.org*
  - *www.entertainmentcareers.net*
- Sample Sides and Scripts (A side is only a portion of a full script)
  - *www.lacasting.com*
  - *www.showfax.com*
- Improv Classes
  - *www.melaniechartoff.com*
- Museum Of Television
  - *www.mtr.org*

Appendix V

Audition Considerations

- Always give yourself a half an hour longer than you think you will need to travel to the audition.

- Count on getting lost or taking extra time to park.

- Get to the audition at least twenty minutes before your sign in time.

- Don't sign in until you are ready to read at your call time.

- Ask questions if you need information—but don't go overboard.

- Focus on your task at hand; don't chat or let others psyche you out.

- Prepare copy several different ways so you won't be thrown by new direction by the casting director or agent.

- Be ready for any set up (low light, etc., in the waiting room).

- Make sure you're physically comfortable.

- Take anything another actor says with a grain of salt.

- Never apologize for your work or emphasize your faults!

- Always leave your troubles at the door.

- Make it a real scene you believe—never just an audition!

- Thank your casting director or agent when you leave.

Appendix VI

Tongue Twisters

Big black bears
Bake brownies while breathing
Back black smoke

Snakes smile so sweetly
When they see shiny
Snails sitting on the
Shore

Thank Theodore for
Those thatched roofs and
Thick thistles without
Thorns, Thaddaeous

Cats catch
Caterpillars' colds
And cough candidly
Can't you hear them cough, cough, cough

She sees shiny shoes
Sundays sometimes
But she sells shields on Saturday

Very vexed vixens
Veer from vipers
When Vivian wears very
Va-va-va-voom velvet

Tick tock take time to
Touch your toes and
Tap twenty times tonight

Nancy never will canoodle with nine
Nasty knob-kneed knights
Now or in the near future

My mother makes macaroons merrily
Mostly in May
When she's marooned munching mulberry muffins

Don't dawdle darling
Deer dash dangerously
Down in this dip in the driveway

Edward edges east early
Egging Ebert
Eerily close to enormous elephants

Foxes find ferries fine
For feathered friends
Fencing fiercely for their fat lives

Gabby goose, grab a good
Gander and get gobbling some
Grain to grow grander for grandfather

Hal hopes Haley
Hasn't heard how
Home-wreckers hover
Hastily on holy holidays ha! ha!

Ingrid inches inward
Inappropriately in
Icy igloos when ice storms ensue

Jerry just jabs John jokingly
As a jest as he jauntily gestures

Kilts keep Ken clean and
Can cluster clans
In cloisters with
Crooked cooks

Let Lenny lean languidly
Lest he'll lose lots of
Lean muscle in long lopsided races

Quick queer questions
Cause the queen to quiver on her quest
For quiet quantum physics solutions

Really royal raisins
Riot raucously when rainy days
Rob them of sunny rays

Uppity urchins under umbrellas
Urge unctuous umpires to usurp
Underhanded underwear salesmen

Appendix VII

Rates

RADIO*
Expires October 29th, 2006

SESSION FEE $235.40
This SESSION FEE is paid for each spot you record. A like amount is paid each 13-WEEK renewal Cycle while in USE.

LA or Chicago Alone 13 - Week "WILD SPOT" USE RATE $319.60
♥ A "WILD SPOT" is for UNLIMITED use in as many cities, on as many stations for any number of airings. When your "WILD SPOT" airs you are paid the USE RATE based on the number and size of those cities.
NOTE: Producers are given, in most cases, one credit for the previously paid SESSION FEE. That SESSION FEE amount is only deducted from the FIRST 13-WEEK USE RATE payment.

ADDITIONAL "TAG" RATE (AT BEGINNING, MIDDLE, OR END)	$97.40
"DEMOS - COPY TESTS FOR NON-AIR" FEE	$162.20
4 - WEEK "NATIONAL NETWORK" USE RATE	$646.15
13 - WEEK "NATIONAL NETWORK" USE RATE	$1,277.20
13 - WEEK "REGIONAL NETWORK" USE RATE	$770.75

BROADCAST TELEVISION*
Expires October 29th, 2006

SESSION FEE $402.25
This SESSION FEE is paid for each spot recorded. A like amount is paid each 13-WEEK renewal Cycle for USE or HOLD (Holding Fee).

LA or Chicago Alone 13 - Week "WILD SPOT" USE RATE $646.30
♥ (Refer to above)

ADDITIONAL "TAGS" *(2-25 IN BODY OF SPOT OR AT END) $119.65

Public Service Announcement "PSA" (w/ SAG waiver) 1-YEAR USE RATE $402.25

"NON-AIR DEMO" FEE $201.15

13 - WEEK "PROGRAM CLASS A / NETWORK" (EACH AIRING) USE RATE $402.25

1ST USE	2ND USE	3-13 USES	14 USES OR MORE
$402.25	$96.00	$76.35 EA.	$34.65 EA.

NETWORK TELEVISION CODE*
Effective through November 15th, 2007

PROMO RATE $227.00
7 DAY RATE for on and off-camera performers in Television Program Promotional Announcements airing on TV or Cable. The 13-Week Rate is $350.00. The Rate when airing on Radio is $270.00 per 13-Weeks.

ADDITIONAL PROMO "TAG" RATE (AT BEGINNING, MIDDLE, OR END) $93.00

SESSION FEES / USE RATES

*Producer contributes up to 14.30% above salary to Actors Pension, Health & Retirement

CABLE TV*

Expires October 29th, 2006

13 - WEEK "COMMERCIAL" RATE $402.25

Minimum RATE for UNLIMITED airings in a 13-WEEK Cycle. A like amount is paid each 13-WEEK renewal Cycle while in USE or on HOLD (Holding Fee), EXCEPT MADE FOR CABLE ONLY where there is NO Holding Fee. A higher RATE could be paid based on a combined total of Cable Subscriber units. The maximum amount of units is approximately 2000 = $1896.50 per 13-WEEK cycle.

NON-BROADCAST-CAT. 1 / INDUSTRIAL / EDUCATIONAL*

Expired June 30, 2005

NARRATION (FIRST HOUR SPENT IN YOUR RECORDING SESSION) (CAT.2 $400.50)	$360.00
NARRATION (EACH ADDITIONAL HALF HOUR INCREMENT OF SESSION)	$105.00
OFF & ON-CAMERA NARRATOR SPOKESPERSON (1ST DAY) (CAT.2 $947.50)	$800.00
NARRATOR SPOKESPERSON (EACH ADDITIONAL DAY) (CAT.2 $547.00)	$440.00

ADR WALLA *

Expires June 30th, 2008

SESSION FEE $716.00

This SESSION FEE is paid for recognizable voicing of five lines or more in a Theatrical Film, MOW, TV Series or Pilot. Residuals are paid based on each airing either Network, Syndication, Cable or Foreign and Video or Multimedia release. These residuals are activated using the same formula as on-camera performers. The voice performer is placed on the CAST LIST.

ANIMATION - TELEVISION ANIMATION *

Expires June 30th, 2008

SESSION FEE $716.00

This SESSION FEE is paid for up to Three Voices in a single program or segments of programs over ten minutes in length. Less than 10 minutes the FEE will be $648.00. If more than Three Voices, you shall be paid an additional $209.00 per voice. Residuals are based on Producers optioned payment schedules.

INTERACTIVE MEDIA *

Effective through December 31st, 2006

DAY PERFORMER RATE $716.00

This Off-Camera RATE is paid for any single Interactive Platform performance of up to Three Voices during a Four Hour Day. Add $238.70 for each additional voice. The Day Performer RATE for 1 voice / 1 hour is $358.00. Voices used on any ON-LINE or NETWORK Platform or used as a 'LIFT' to another program, add an additional 100% of the original RATE in each case if the rights are acquired within one year of initial release and 110% after such period.

AUDIOBOOK *

All Rates are Per Hour (in studio) or Per Side, whichever is higher

NARRATOR / ANNOUNCER	$145.00
ACTOR (1 ROLE)	$127.75
ACTOR (2 ROLES)	$255.50
ACTOR (3+ ROLES)	$385.00

For these purposes AFTRA has defined a Side as
"each 5-minute segment of (your finished product) recorded material
on which the artist respectively performs."

33

Suggested Readings

Adler, Stella. *The Technique Of Acting.* New York: Bantam Books, 1988. Boston: Focal Press, 2002.

Alburger, James R. *The Art of Voice Acting: The Craft and Business of Performing Voice Over.* Boston: Focal Press, 2002.

Berland, Terry and Ouellette, Deborah. *Breaking Into Commercials.* New York: Silman-James Press, 2006.

Blu, Susan; Mullin, Molly Ann; and Songé, Cynthia. *Word of Mouth: A Guide to Commercial Voice Over Excellence.* Los Angeles: Silman-James Press, 2006.

Caine, Michael. *Acting in Film: An Actor's Take on Movie Making.* New York: Applause Acting Series, 1997.

Cameron, Julia. *Heart Steps: Prayers and Declarations for a Creative Life.* New York: Jeremy P. Tarcher/Putnam, 1997.

Cameron, Julia. *Supplies: A Pilot's Guide to Creative Flight.* New York: Jeremy P. Tarcher/Putnam, 2000.

Cameron, Julia. *The Artist's Way: A Spiritual Path to Higher Creativity.* New York: Jeremy P. Tarcher/Putnam, 2002.

Cameron, Julia. *Walking in This World: The Practical Art of Creativity.* New York: Jeremy P. Tarcher/Putnam, 2002.

Carnegie, Dale. *How to Win Friends & Influence People.* New York: Pocket Books, 1998.

Cartwright, Nancy. *My Life As A Ten-Year-Old Boy: Voice of Bart Simpson.* New York: Hyperion, 2000.

Chubbuck, Ivana. *The Power of the Actor: The Chubbuck Technique.* New York: Gotham Books, 2004.

Fisher, Jeffrey P. and Hogan, Harlan. *The Voice Actor's Guide to Home Recording.* Boston: Thomson Course Technology PTR, 2005.

Gitomer, Jeffrey H. *Jeffrey Gitomer's Little Red Book of Selling: 12.5 Principles of Sales Greatness: How to Make Sales Forever.* Austin: Bard Press, 2004.

Hagen, Uta, with Frankel, Haskel. *Respect for Acting.* New York: Macmillan Publishing, 1973.

Hogan, Harlan. *VO: Tales and Techniques of a Voice-over Actor.* New York: Allworth Press, 2002.

Hooks, Ed. *The Audition Book: Winning Strategies for Breaking into Theatre, Film, and Television.* New York: Backstage Books, 1989.

Karshner, Roger. *You Said a Mouthful: Tongue Twisters to Tangle, Titillate, Test, and Tease.* Toluca Lake, CA: Dramaline Publications, 1993.

Manderino, Ned. *All About Method Acting*. Los Angeles: Maderino Books, 1985.

Meisner, Sanford. *Sanford Meisner on Acting*. New York: Vintage Books, Inc., 1987.

Olivier, Laurence. *Confessions of an Actor: An Autobiography*. New York: Simon and Schuster, 1982.

Saulsberry, Rodney. *You Can Bank on Your Voice*. Agoura Hills, CA: Tomdor Publications, 2004.

Schiffman, Stephan. *The 25 Sales Habits of Highly Successful Salespeople*. Holbrook, MA: B. Adams, 1994.

Shurtleff, Michael. *Audition: Everything an Actor Needs to Know to Get the Part*. New York: Bantam Books, 1980.

Smith, Marisa and Schewel, Amy. *The Actor's Book of Movie Monologues*. New York: Penguin Books, 1986.

Spolin, Viola *Improvisation for the Theatre: A Handbook of Teaching and Directing Techniques*, Third Edition. Evanston, IL: Northwestern University Press, 2000.

Warhit, Doug. *Book the Job: 143 Things Actors Need to Know to Make it Happen*. Los Angeles: Dau Publishing, 2003.

About the CD

The CD that supplements this book is divided into four tracks. The first track is a collection of warm-ups, and exercises for improving relaxation, breathing, articulation, and vocal technique. The remaining three tracks are interviews with successful voice actors Michael Yurchak, John Matthew, and Melanie Chartoff. Their biographies can be found below.

MICHAEL YURCHAK is an improvisor and actor, living in Los Angeles with his wife, Molly, and their son, Luca (15 months). Michael is currently on the air as the voice of Ben, Adelbert, and Isaac on PBS Kids' *News Flash Five*, and can also be heard as a regular arts and entertainment voice on NY 1 in New York City. He has been a featured voice in many commercials including current spots for Wendy's, Stop & Shop, and Continental Tires.

This was a banner year for Michael, as his voice-over characters hit the big screen with Hollywood stars. He had roles in *Broken Lizard's Beerfest* with Cloris Leachman and Will Forte, *Watching the Detectives* starring Lucy Liu and Cillian Murphy, and *The Lather Effect* featuring Eric Stoltz and Ione Skye. Look for them in theaters and video stores near you!

Michael received his master's degree from New York University. He enjoys teaching as well as working as a voice-over artist and actor. His own work has taken an educational spin lately, as he voiced the main character for Educate Inc.'s *Hooked-On* series, teaching children to speak Spanish, French, and even Chinese! As a new father, his work is more enjoyable for him when he knows it may be valuable to young people.

JOHN MATTHEW did his first voice-over job at age 6 and took a 20-year hiatus before returning to the recording booth. In the interim, he learned to play the piano, drums, and guitar. He exhausted himself with volleyball, rollerblading, and mountain climbing before he returned to the profession that required the least running.

Now a veteran with over 15 years in the business, John has lent his voice to hundreds of projects in all types of media, from radio to the Internet. He has narrated over forty-five episodes of the Food Network Challenge, as well as "The History of The Beach" for the History Channel, and several special features in the Star Wars Trilogy DVD boxed set. Most recently, John was the promo voice for *The Montel Williams Show*, featured in two Jack-In-The-Box radio spots, and the announcer on infomercials for *Core Rhythms* and *Carnie Wilson's Lite and Hope*.

In addition to voicing, producing, and editing demos for other voice actors, John continues to play guitar, upgrade his studio, and crack wise at social gatherings. A self-described "Local Personality," John now enjoys enough political clout to write his own bios. (*www.johnmatthew.com*)

MELANIE CHARTOFF considers herself an inventor of stories and characters for the page, stage and screen, as well as for environmental issues, having patented a graywater recycling device for home use (*graywayrotatingdrain.com*). As an actress, she's most recently been seen in the season finale of *Desperate Housewives* and in last season's long-running *Sunset Park* at the Zephyr Theater in Hollywood. She won a Dramalogue Award for *March of the Falsettoes* and acclaim for her performances in productions such as ACT San Francisco's *Sunday in the Park with George*, *The Vagina Monologues* in Chicago, and *Beyond Therapy* at the Coronet Theater in Los Angeles. She can be heard daily as the voice of Didi and Minka on Nickleodeon's long-running *Rugrats* and its spin-off *All Grown Up*, as well as the accompanying movies and CD-ROMs.

Melanie is best known for her diverse roles in series television such as ABC's late night comedy show *Fridays, Parker Lewis Can't Lose, The Newhart Show, Ally McBeal*, and *Touched by an Angel*. She hails from the East Coast stages of Long Wharf Theater, Yale, off-off, off, and on Broadway. She currently "charismatizes" people in her Improvisational Presence and School for the Shy Workshops at the Hayworth Theater in Hollywood. (*www.melaniechartoff.com*)

About the Author

I didn't really enjoy every game I played as a child, but I was raised with a very competitive spirit to achieve. This came in handy as I studied for my master's degree in Communications from the Annenberg School at the University of Pennsylvania. My book may also be influenced by my first staff job working for Emmy-Award winning, Olympic Sports Producer Bud Greenspan. I do know I have always been fascinated with physical feats and loved the very competitive spirit of dance.

HBO was where I really learned to play in the business as a promo writer/producer and got to direct segments with celebrities like Colleen Dewhurst, O.J. Simpson, and Jerry Seinfeld. At HBO I was asked to do my first voice-over and then studied and benefited from the encouragement and employment from my peers. I also was cheered on to pursue acting full out in the very creative scene where I worked.

I studied singing in New York to keep my voice in shape. Paul Sills was a teacher who really taught me the joy of being in the moment and being playful with acting. I learned that games are a terrific tool to trick the mind into using the imagination in a natural way. This guided me through Repertory Theatre, an Improv Show in a comedy club, and all my film and TV work.

Landing a weekly gig doing the Lifetime Billboards gave me the freedom to breathe as a mother and devote more time to acting. Moving to Los Angeles, I was forced to adapt and bend to the changing voice-over world and learn how to use a home studio. Doing the live voice-over for AMC's *Nicole Kidman, An American Cinematheque Tribute*, tested new chops and was so much fun. It took me back to my first job announcing over the public announce system at the county fair when I was in high school.

In contrast, my narration of the one-hour E! Show, *Hollywood & Divine: Beauty Secrets Revealed*, let me create a playful character with attitude á la the narrator on the show *Desperate Housewives*.

Teaching voice-over at UCLA Extension enabled me to bring all my experience together in a fun way. I found that using games to break up work at the mic really helped students grow. This book is an attempt to capture my class work and I hope you can enjoy the creative and playful spirit of pursuing a voice-over career.

Index

Books from Allworth Press

Allworth Press is an imprint of Allworth Communications, Inc. Selected titles are listed below.

VO: Tales and Techniques of a Voice-Over Actor
by *Harlan Hogan* (paperback, 6 × 9, 256 pages, $19.95)

The Actor's Other Career Book: Using Your Chops to Survive and Thrive
by *Lisa Mulcahy* (paperback, 6 × 9, 256 pages, $19.95)

How to Audition for TV Commercials: From the Ad Agency Point of View
by *W. L. Jenkins* (paperback, 6 × 9, 208 pages, $16.95)

Acting—Advanced Techniques for the Actor, Director, and Teacher
by *Terry Schreiber* (paperback, 6 × 9, 256 pages, $19.95)

The Art of Auditioning: Techniques for Television
by *Rob Decina* (paperback, 6 × 9, 224 pages, $19.95)

Promoting Your Acting Career: A Step-by-Step Guide to Opening the Right Doors, Second Edition
by *Glenn Alterman* (paperback, 6 × 9, 240 pages, $19.95)

The Actor Rehearses: What to Do When and Why
by *David Hlavsa* (paperback, 6 × 9, 2224 pages, $18.95)

The Actor's Way: A Journey of Self-Discovery in Letters
by *Benjamin Lloyd* (paperback, 5½ × 8½, 224 pages, $16.95)

Acting Is a Job: Real Life Lessons about the Acting Business
by *Jason Pugatch* (paperback, 6 × 9, 240 pages, $19.95)

Please write to request our free catalog. To order by credit card, call 1-800-491-2808 or send a check or money order to Allworth Press, 10 East 23rd Street, Suite 510, New York, NY 10010. Include $6 for shipping and handling for the first book ordered and $1 for each additional book. Ten dollars plus $1 for each additional book if ordering from Canada. New York State residents must add sales tax.

To see our complete catalog on the World Wide Web, or to order online, you can find us at ***www.allworth.com.***